HOSTING A LIBRARY MYSTERY

HOSTING A LIBRARY MYSTERY

A Programming Guide

Elizabeth M. Karle

AMERICAN LIBRARY ASSOCIATION
CHICAGO 2009

ELIZABETH M. KARLE received a B.A. in business administration and finance from the University of Notre Dame, a paralegal certificate from Roosevelt University, and an M.A. in library and information science from Dominican University. She is currently the collection management supervisor for the Cushwa-Leighton Library at Saint Mary's College in Notre Dame, Indiana.

Library of Congress Cataloging-in-Publication Data
Karle, Elizabeth M.
  Hosting a library mystery : a programming guide / Elizabeth M. Karle.
  p. cm.
  Includes bibliographical references and index.
  ISBN 978-0-8389-0986-7 (alk. paper)
  1. Libraries—Activity programs. 2. Library orientation. 3. Mystery games.
  I. Title.
  Z716.33.K37 2009
  025.5—dc22   2008052524

ISBN-13: 978-0-8389-0986-7

Printed in the United States of America

13 12 11 10 09   5 4 3 2 1

For my parents,

with eternal love and gratitude

xoxox

CONTENTS

ACKNOWLEDGMENTS

Writing a book is a labor of love. There is so much time, energy, research, preparation, and attention to detail involved that you have to care deeply about your subject to want to share the information or story. You also need to have a strong support system around you—before, during, and after the project is completed. Without key people, the work would be neither worthwhile nor fun; worse, you may find you are not qualified to do the job, or it simply might never get done.

Clearly, then, there are numerous people connected with me or with this book whom I need to recognize. Thank you, first and foremost, to Janet Fore, director of the Cushwa-Leighton Library at Saint Mary's College. Without her vision and encouragement, I never would have undertaken this endeavor. My gratitude goes out to Sister Bernice Hollenhorst too, for giving me the opportunity and for her continued support.

I cannot say enough about my colleagues in the library who not only motivate me, but literally make it possible for us to host mystery events. Extra-special thanks are due to Jill Hobgood, Bob Hohl, Catherine Pellegrino, and Janet Fore for all of their help and reference assistance. We have had a few late nights! In the "Characters, Props, Costumes and 'Whatever Else You Need' Department," I could not have pulled together these mysteries without a lot of input from Brittany Collins, Aaron "Gus" Dahman, Karen Hobgood, Bob Hohl, Michael Kelly, Catherine Pittman, Carol Rafferty, and Jamie Rathert-Dahman. And the evenings would not have been nearly as much fun without the presence of Rosalind Clark, Chris Cobb, Nichole Fundora, Hannah Monroe, Melinda Pittman, Kate Ward, and Whit Young.

Of course, I need to mention the wonderful cooperation the library received from the Saint Mary's College Security, Building Services, and Special Events departments. And thank you to Sodexho Food Services for catering our events and giving them a special touch.

I owe a debt of gratitude to the folks at ALA Editions, especially my editor, Stephanie Zvirin, and Jill Davis, Beverly Miller, and Eugenia Chun. They made the entire process a smooth one. It was a pleasure working together.

Finally, I extend my affection and appreciation to those who are most important to me: to my parents, Tom and Madreen, for instilling in me a passion for learning, for fostering my endless curiosity, and for accepting me for who I am; to my siblings, Thom, Meeghan, and Christen, who, along with Tyler, Jack, Grace, Maddie, and Karle, not only believe in me, but also nurture my imagination and keep it alive; to Carol, on whose love and support I rely and to whom I am indebted; to the Bertacchini, Bernardi, Bogan, Fiocchi, and Karle relations with whom I was blessed to have grown up—their words and examples inspired me and impressed on me the importance of education, reading, and libraries; to Tory, Arri, and Melinda, for bringing the Ninja Turtles, Robin Hood, the Pigs-in-the-Wigs, Hogwarts, and many other adventures to life for me along the way; and to Catherine, whose love and understanding make a good team even better, and whose playfulness started me down this mysterious path with a note in a book one day.

INTRODUCTION

The most beautiful and deepest
experience a man can have is the sense
of the mysterious. It is the underlying
principle of religion as well as all
serious endeavor in art and science.
—Albert Einstein, 1932

Welcome to the world of library mysteries! If you are involved in programming, outreach, or instruction for your library, this book is for you. In it, you will find instructions and examples to help you create an entertaining event through which your patrons can engage in active learning.

Mystery events can serve many purposes. A mystery can be presented as an orientation to the library and its staff members. It can provide the framework for a tour of the library's facilities. Mysteries can act as introductions to resources the library possesses or serve as a timely review of research skills for more experienced patrons. Mysteries can be teaching tools, and they should be fun. Good mysteries excite patrons, generating interest in the library as well as positioning it as a friendly, welcoming place to explore.

In 2002, the Friends of the Gould Library at Carleton College in Northfield, Minnesota, hosted a murder mystery as a promotional event for their students. This special evening was such a success that they posted "How to Host a Murder Mystery . . . in Your Library" on the college's website.[1] Inspired by this concept, I set out to write mysteries for the Cushwa-Leighton Library at Saint Mary's College in Notre Dame, Indiana. To date, we have hosted six mysteries with different topics, styles, and functions. The photographs from these events that are inserted throughout this book show how intently the patrons are participating—as well as how much everyone is enjoying the experience.

This book contains scripts for mysteries, most hosted at Saint Mary's College, as well as instructions and tips for staging a successful mystery event. By their nature, these mysteries are meant to be adapted to your particular library, be it an academic, public, or school library. You will need to consider your library's resources and make modifications, taking into account your holdings and what you are trying to accomplish.

Mysteries can require different skill sets in addition to knowledge of library resources. I have included mysteries that incorporate puzzles and word games. Others consist of clues that require detection and deduction. Often characters are involved, and the staff becomes part of the event by portraying the characters. One mystery was designed for a specific academic discipline. These examples can serve as guides; the possibilities for your library mystery are limited only by your imagination.

The purpose of this book is not only to get the wheels turning, but also to suggest a variety of shapes your mystery can take. The resources section sets out links to mysteries hosted by other libraries and thereby provides you with even more ideas.

Think you might have trouble selling the idea of a mystery event to your director? As I stated in my article "Invigorating the Library Experience," now, more than ever before, improving a library's ability to engage its patrons while positively shaping their perceptions is vital to the completion of the library's mission. Establishing the image of librarians as user friendly is critical to revitalizing patrons' library experiences.[2]

You also might refer to "A Library Adventure: Comparing a Treasure Hunt with a Traditional Freshman Orientation Tour," by Sandra Marcus and Sheila Beck. As part of their study, they used a mystery format in their treasure hunt (they include the text in their article). Their research demonstrated "the need for continuing experimentation, innovation, and creativity in orientation tour design, as well as the value of such introductory tours, enhancing both comfort level and skill in library use."[3] This conclusion reinforces the idea that learning packaged in a novel way makes a positive impression on patrons.

At a time when libraries are competing against a variety of technological innovations and amusements, organizations that market their resources in an engaging manner will be the most successful. And while library mysteries do educate as they entertain, they are serious business as well. As Einstein implies, mystery is inherent in almost any discipline or area of interest. A mystery event therefore can be an exploration of any topic or branch of learning you choose.

This book sets out some behind-the-scenes preparations and procedures to follow in order to showcase your library's resources for inquiring minds. Chapters 1 through 3 provide an illustrative, step-by step explanation of the process used to develop one specific mystery hosted by Saint Mary's College. Chapter 4 explains how libraries can adapt mystery scripts that others have used. Chapter 5 offers overall logistical considerations and a checklist to use when planning your own mystery event. The remaining chapters provide scripts for several mysteries that serve a variety of functions, contain an assortment of clues and methods, and illustrate a number of possible mystery designs.

All of the material presented here is to be adapted to suit your library's needs. You will see that there are no right or wrong methods, just suggestions, examples, and a flair for the dramatic.

NOTES

1. www.carleton.edu/campus/library/reference/workshops/MurderMystery.html.
2. Elizabeth M. Karle, "Invigorating the Library Experience: Creative Programming Ideas," *College and Research Libraries News* 69, no. 3 (March 2008): 141–144.
3. Sandra Marcus and Sheila Beck, "A Library Adventure: Comparing a Treasure Hunt with a Traditional Freshman Orientation Tour," *College and Research Libraries* 64, no. 1 (January 2003): 23–44.

PART ONE

WRITING, PREPARING, AND HOSTING

Chapters 1 through 5 contain information on creating, adapting, and hosting mystery events. The step-by-step approach walks through the construction of a mystery script. This is followed by a discussion of how this script can be modified for use by another library. Special considerations for planning and staging mystery events are addressed as well.

CHAPTER ONE

WHERE TO BEGIN

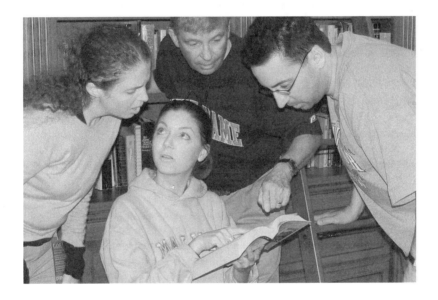

The first consideration when writing the script for a mystery is the purpose of the event—for example:

- to orient patrons to the library's facilities
- to educate patrons about the library's collections
- to give patrons experience using the library's online resources
- to introduce patrons to a newly acquired resource
- to plan an engaging event for patrons
- to promote the library to a specific audience
- to acquaint patrons with library staff members
- to present resources in a specific discipline
- to include as an adjunct to a social studies or history course
- to review skills for those previously acquainted with library resources

- to create a friendly competition between groups (e.g., faculty and students)
- to offer a summer reading program alternative that's fun
- to provide an event related to a current topic of interest
- to celebrate an event or milestone

Of course, more than one of these motives can apply for a single event. The rationale for the event is important in helping to choose the aspects of the library to highlight, as well as the skills to reinforce when writing clues.

The next consideration is a theme: the subject around which the mystery is built. Once a theme is in place, your research into the subject will take you in various directions, with many potential avenues to pursue with clues and characters.

In selecting a theme, think about the purpose of the mystery. If it is about a current event, milestone, or specific resource, you will have some good possibilities. Perhaps it is the library's twenty-fifth anniversary, or Valentine's Day, or a prominent speaker is coming to town. Maybe your library just purchased the multivolume *The Birds of North America* or you offer Rosetta Stone software. Ornithology, state birds, country profiles, and modern languages are good topic ideas to highlight these resources.

If the purpose of the mystery is an orientation or involves more library-specific procedures, you can still embark on something creative. Consider well-known books or movies as themes, such as Harry Potter or *The Wizard of Oz*. Take into account where your library is located. Do history, sports, nature, or folklore figure prominently in your area? In San Francisco, you might choose the gold rush. In Chicago, perhaps a sports theme would be fun. The Revolutionary War and the Appalachian Trail provide lots of topic ideas along the East Coast. Is there something in which your patrons share a particular interest, such as poetry? Maybe you want to create original characters and settings of your own. A public library might want to host a mystery specifically for patrons who regularly read mysteries.

Do not be afraid to take a risk. Even seemingly obscure themes will lead to plenty of resources and research possibilities. Ask your coworkers and patrons for suggestions. Good themes will pique patron curiosity and serve as a means of telling a story. The important thing is to be imaginative and have fun with the topic.

To provide a useful example, let's examine the script from a mystery hosted at Saint Mary's College in April 2007. Saint Mary's is a Catholic women's liberal arts college in Notre Dame, Indiana, whose mascot is the Belles. For the theme, we chose to investigate "famous belles." One intriguing possibility was to research the life of Belle Starr, a female outlaw in the late 1800s. This reference to the college's mascot was also a good tie-in for publicity purposes. We entitled our mystery "A Belle Gone Wild" to attract the students' attention. Let's walk through this mystery step-by-step as an illustration.

In "A Belle Gone Wild," our motivation for doing the mystery was to orient our patrons, the students, to the library's facilities, as well as to expose them to the library's collections. We also wanted to give them experience using our online resources, and, of course, we wanted them to have fun. So in our preparation, we knew we wanted the students to succeed at the following tasks:

- Use the online catalog to look up a book, note the call number, and find that book in the stacks.
- Gain experience searching online resources such as JSTOR, WorldCat, and Academic Search Premier.
- Interact with the reference librarian and other staff members.
- Locate a print article in the periodicals section.
- Ask for an item on reserve.
- Know where to find the elevator, photocopier, audiovisual section, restroom, book drop, and other areas in the building.

Once our goals were established, we moved on to consider the nature of the mystery. Would it be a whodunit? Was something stolen? Did someone disappear? Were the participants trying to find factual information? Attempting to solve a puzzle? Learning more about a subject area? There were many possibilities, which could include real or imaginary characters. In the Belle Starr event, a fictional history professor, Dr. Ima Gonner, was "missing," and the students had to determine her whereabouts.

The mystery thus began to take shape. We knew what subject we were going to research and the ultimate question to be answered: Where is the missing professor? Next we needed to weave together our goals and our resources to create a set of clues. This is where our skill as researchers and our creativity came together.

Consider the first goal: using the online catalog to find a book in the stacks. A search of Saint Mary's catalog did not reveal any book specifically about Belle Starr. But we were not discouraged; this was not a dead end. We did find *The Women*, in The Old West series, by the editors of Time-Life Books. A quick check of the index showed that Belle Starr is mentioned on several pages. We set this book aside for future reference.

While doing this search on the Old West, we also saw that Saint Mary's owns a reference book entitled *Cowboys and the Wild West*. Belle Starr is mentioned in this book too, so we pulled it as well.

The next goal was providing experience using online resources. We knew that there must be articles and books written about Belle Starr. Saint Mary's subscribes to many periodical journals and e-journals, so we searched for Belle Starr in WorldCat. Success! We found an article with an amusing, and rather long, title:

At last for the discriminating reader, an unvarnished, straight-shooting, and instructive account of the wild, wild West: containing the irreducible,

> rock-bottom, and unadorned facts about such desperadoes, sheriffs, gun slingers, cowtown marshals, and assorted riffraff as Wild Bill Hickok, Bat Masterson, Wyatt Earp, Billy the Kid, and Jesse James; together with various moral lessons and scandalous tales about their fair but frail companions Calamity Jane and Belle Starr

The article is by Peter Lyon. A number of other books and articles on Belle Starr were also listed in WorldCat, so we copied the citations and continued our research.

JSTOR, a full-text database of all but the past two to five years of core scholarly journals within the social sciences and humanities, seemed a likely source of information. We investigated and discovered that a historian named Glenn Shirley wrote two books on our subject: *Belle Starr and Her Times: The Literature, the Facts, and the Legends* and *Outlaw Queen: The Fantastic True Story of Belle Starr, the Most Notorious Gun-Girl in the West*. There also was a review of this first book online in the November 1983 issue of the *Journal of Southern History* that we printed out.

Further investigation in the online periodical index Academic Search Premier revealed "Belle Starr: the Bandit Queen," an article in *College and Research Libraries News*. Saint Mary's carries the full text of that periodical in print, another useful source. There also was an entry for an article entitled "The Man Who Knew Belle Starr," by Richard Bausch, from 1987. We saved that reference too.

By this point, we had many potential avenues to pursue. We had chosen a theme loosely based on the college's mascot and found a good amount of information. Best of all, it was only the tip of the iceberg! Continuing our research provided us with lots of information, facts, and even photos to help us put our mystery in context. We formed a working theory: Dr. Ima Gonner, a history professor, studies Belle Starr. She was doing research when she disappeared. Where did she go? We reviewed the resources we collected and came up with a plausible explanation that became the crux of our mystery: the solution our patrons must determine. Then we formulated the clues to lead them in the right direction. Along the way, they learned about our library and all it has to offer.

CHAPTER TWO

BUILDING THE FRAMEWORK

We needed to determine Dr. Ima Gonner's whereabouts. Evaluating the information we discovered about Belle Starr, the historian Glenn Shirley stood out, since he wrote two books about her. Coincidently, Belle Starr's maiden name was Shirley; their common surname could be a helpful clue. We did not use it, but it could lead to a clue or red herring for someone else. Delving further into Glenn Shirley's background, we found that there is a Glenn D. Shirley Western Americana Collection at the National Cowboy Museum in Oklahoma City, Oklahoma. Bingo! We concluded that Dr. Gonner went there to do research. We now had our destination and the answer to our mystery.

We began to work toward this conclusion by turning to the clues. One thing to remember when selecting details to use in clues is to hang on to your source information. Printed citations are helpful. You will need this information in the future if you have to answer any questions or make any adjustments to the script. You also will use factors such as call numbers to help place some of the clues within the library.

Writing clues is another area where creativity comes into play. Keep in mind the goals and the tasks you want your patrons to perform. In our mystery, we wanted to convey some interesting information about Belle Starr while leading the students to Dr. Ima Gonner's whereabouts.

Remember that there is no right or wrong way to write the clues. They are merely a means to an end. Some may have greater significance than others; perhaps some will be red herrings. Some can lead directly to a location or resource, or be used indirectly to influence the flow of the event. Generally it is better to have more information prepared than you need, because that gives you flexibility.

We looked back through some of our research (outlined in chapter 1) and consulted the book from the Old West Time-Life series. The following sentence from *The Women* seemed to be good material for a clue:

- "Belle was the brains behind a gang of cattle thieves in the Oklahoma Territory."
  Source: call number HQ 1418 .T58

From the reference book *Cowboys and the Wild West,* we noted:

- Belle Starr born was born in Carthage, Missouri.
  Source: call number REF F 596 .C97 1994

According to *Women in U.S. History: A Resource Guide:*

- *High Spirited Women of the West* by Anne Seagraves, which includes a biography of Belle Starr.
  Source: Call number REF HQ 1410 .H36

At this stage, we were looking at the resources we had found on our topic and picking out interesting facts and items that seemed to lend themselves to being clues. We could choose to use different aspects of the information in the actual clue: an author's name, a location, a call number, or a title, for example. The clues would then be expressed as questions derived from these items. At this stage, they were random tidbits, like colors on a paint palette. We moved on to think about what else we could use.

We wanted to incorporate that wonderfully outrageous title by Peter Lyon:

- "At last for the discriminating reader, an unvarnished, straight-shooting, and instructive account of the wild, wild West: containing the irreducible, rock-bottom, and unadorned facts about such desperadoes, sheriffs, gun slingers, cowtown marshals, and assorted riffraff as Wild Bill Hickok, Bat Masterson, Wyatt Earp, Billy the Kid, and Jesse James; together with various moral lessons and scandalous tales about their fair but frail companions Calamity Jane and Belle Starr"
  Source: WorldCat

We also needed to include information about Glenn Shirley. We could combine that with an online database search and perhaps an interlibrary loan request:

- Glenn Shirley's book *Belle Starr and Her Times: The Literature, the Facts, and the Legends* was reviewed by Richard E. Meyer in the November 1983 issue of the *Journal of Southern History.*
  Source: JSTOR

- Only nine libraries carry the book *Outlaw Queen: The Fantastic True Story of Belle Starr, the Most Notorious Gun-Girl in the West* by Glenn Shirley. They are located in California, Oklahoma, New Mexico, Colorado, and Texas.
  Source: WorldCat

One of our goals was to have the patrons to locate an article in the bound and current periodicals sections of our library, so we added:

- The June 2005 issue of *College and Research Libraries News* (volume 66, no. 6, p. 483), which includes a review of the book *Belle Starr: The Bandit Queen.*
  Source: Academic Search Premier

- *Atlantic* published an article written by Richard Bausch, "The Man Who Knew Belle Starr," in its April 1987 issue (volume 259, no. 4).
  Source: Academic Search Premier

We wanted our patrons to find the library's audiovisual (A/V) section. We had not yet addressed audiovisual media in our research, but a quick check of the catalog revealed that Saint Mary's owns a video of the musical *Oklahoma!:*

- The call number for *Oklahoma!* is A/V PN 1997 .O41
  Source: catalog

Sifting through other information, we found a book review written in 1987 by a nun stating, "This book will probably suit readers of torrid paperback romances." That was just too good a quote not to incorporate. We could print a copy of the review. Again, keeping in mind our goals, we considered placing this review on reserve.

- The book entitled *Belle Starr: A Novel of the Old West* by Deborah Camp was reviewed in *Library Journal* by Sister Avila of the Academy of the Holy Angels in Minneapolis, Minnesota, in 1987.
  Source: Academic Search Premier

We collected additional information through our research in chapter 1 that we might use:

- Belle Starr served six months at the Detroit House of Corrections in Detroit, Michigan, in 1883.
  Source: AllExperts.com encyclopedia entry

- Richard K. Fox wrote *Bella Starr, the Bandit Queen; or, the Female Jesse James* in 1889.
  Source: Infoplease.com entry—www.infoplease.com

- Belle Starr's given name was Myra Belle Shirley.
  Source: Encyclopaedia Britannica entry—www.britannica.com

From our research, we had isolated informative and helpful facts and highlighted the library's resources. Now we needed to use them to write clues to help our patrons find Dr. Gonner.

There is no hard-and-fast rule for how many clues are needed for a good mystery. Some elements to consider are the number of teams or participants in the mystery event, how long you want the event to take, whether you covered all of your goals, and how much detail you need to include about the subject matter.

Some clues are more difficult to solve than others, and some patrons move more quickly through the clues than others. For the Belle Starr mystery, we wrote twelve clues and developed two puzzles. The entire event, from introduction through prize distribution at the end, lasted just over two hours. The other mystery scripts in this book contain different numbers of clues. Flexibility and adaptation will help you to determine the right number. As you prepare the event, though, it is better to gather lots of information in order to write clues that help the event to flow smoothly. It is possible, too, that you will come to a point where you feel you need a specific clue to suit your purposes. At that time, you can do more research about your topic to find exactly what you are looking for.

We used a couple of extra devices in the Belle Starr mystery—a crossword puzzle and an anagram—for variety. This isn't necessary in a mystery script, but since we did it for this mystery, we include it in the instructions in the next chapter. At this point, with specific information selected, you can generate the script for the mystery. The script is the plan that will be followed from beginning to end.

—

Think about the type of event you want to create. The mystery could take the form of a team competition. It might involve individuals role playing, as in the mystery dinner party format. Or perhaps it will be set up more like a tour for individuals to complete at their own pace. Examples of all of these and other types of mysteries are addressed later in this book.

The original purpose of the event is important in determining how the clues will be presented to the patrons. Our motives in the Belle Starr mystery were to get the students to use some of the library's resources and become more familiar with the library's facilities. Since our students had varying levels of experience, we presented this as a team competition, but we did not want it to get out of hand. Six teams of five students allowed us to keep the teams from crossing paths too often while ensuring that each team member participated. And because we wanted to provide prizes and refreshments at the end, thirty students kept us within our budget. Moreover, it was a reasonable number of students to expect for a weekend event on a small campus.

We began by creating a grid in table format to keep track of where each team would be during the course of the event. This was helpful not only in

TABLE 2.1
Initial Grid for the Belle Starr Mystery

BLUE	RED	YELLOW	GREEN	BLACK	ORANGE

TABLE 2.2
Grid Showing the Location of Each Team's First Clue

BLUE	RED	YELLOW	GREEN	BLACK	ORANGE
Elevator	Elevator	Book Drop	Book Drop	Photocopier	Photocopier

making sure the teams arrived at the clues separately, but also in judging the pace at which the teams were proceeding while the event was in progress. The grids were only for staff use; the teams never saw them. We could use thematic designations, such as the Outlaws or the Rustlers. Or team members could choose their own team names. We designated the teams by colors (see table 2.1).

Our mystery began at the circulation desk, which is on the main floor of the library, near the entrance. After a brief introduction, the teams received packets that included instructions. We note where this information directs each team to go on the grid in table 2.2.

Since it was their first clue and they did not have to do any research, sending multiple teams to the same location on the main floor does not

TABLE 2.3

Location and Sequence of all Clues for the Blue Team

BLUE	RED	YELLOW	GREEN	BLACK	ORANGE
Elevator	Elevator	Book Drop	Book Drop	Photocopier	Photocopier
Lower level					
2nd RR					
Photocopier					
Atlantic					
HQ 1418					
Ref lib					
REF F 596					
Reserve					
Book drop					
Video					
Atlas					

give anything away or offer any team an advantage. The clue itself was in an envelope with the color of the team written on it. You may choose to use colored dots, stickers, or some other method of identifying each team's clues. Just remember that if you plan to host the mystery at night and turn the lights off, you want the envelopes to be easily distinguishable.

There were specific areas where the teams needed to go to find their clues: the bound periodicals on lower level, the current periodicals on the main floor, the reserve desk, the reference collection, the HQ section of the general collection, and the A/V section. We also wanted to be sure that they interacted with the reference librarian and found various locations within the building.

The first column of the grid can be filled in with all of the locations where you want the teams to go. This can be in random order, or in a specific order if you know one clue must lead to another. We used abbreviations for the different areas and clues. (See table 2.3.)

We filled in the rest of the table one column at a time, putting each team in a different location as they proceeded through the event. This helped us to chart their progress. There are times when it is okay if some teams are scheduled to be at the same place at the same time. Using an even number of teams helps to keep this to a minimum. Remember that the teams will

TABLE 2.4

Completed Grid Detailing the Locations
and Sequence of Each Team's Clues

BLUE	RED	YELLOW	GREEN	BLACK	ORANGE
Elevator	Elevator	Book drop	Book drop	Photocopier	Photocopier
Lower Level	HQ 1418	Reserve	REF F 596	Video	Atlantic
2nd RR	Photocopier	HQ 1418	Lower level	Reserve	Video
Photocopier	2nd RR	Ref Lib	Elevator	Lower level	Book drop
Atlantic	Video	Lower level	Reserve	2nd RR	Ref Lib
HQ 1418	REF F 596	Photocopier	Video	Atlantic	Reserve
Ref lib	Lower Level	2nd RR	Photocopier	REF F 596	HQ 1418
REF F 596	Reserve	Atlantic	HQ 1418	Ref Lib	2nd RR
Reserve	Ref Lib	Elevator	Atlantic	Book drop	Lower level
Book drop	Atlantic	Video	Ref Lib	Elevator	REF F 596
Video	Book drop	REF F 596	2nd RR	HQ 1418	Elevator
Atlas	Atlas	Atlas	Atlas	Atlas	Atlas

move through the clues at different speeds. In the chart, we noted where the actual envelope would be located in the library. Multiple teams could be in the reference area doing research at the same time, since we had enough computers.

Table 2.4 shows the completed grid.

By comparing each succeeding column with the first column, we could be sure that each team visited every location and that teams overlapped only at the beginning in this example. The framework for our mystery was now in place. In the next chapter, the clues are linked to the locations, and you will see how the mystery flows.

CHAPTER THREE

PUTTING IT ALL TOGETHER

In some mysteries, the clues lead from one to the next in a fixed order. In those cases, teams arrive at the same location in close proximity to one another. In the Belle Starr mystery, the clues were not dependent on one another, so the locations were in random order. And in this case, the manner in which the clues were presented to the teams became important. It was necessary to give directions with some of the clues to tell the teams where to go next. Since our goal was to expose our patrons to the library and its resources, we were careful not to provide the teams with too much of an opportunity to split up in an effort to get ahead. In other types of mystery events, speed might be more advantageous. In those cases, the ingenious teams that compete strategically will look for occasions to get such an advantage.

Our mystery began at the circulation desk on the main floor of the library, near the entrance. The head reference librarian, wearing a cowboy hat and a bolo tie, agreed to give an introduction to the teams. Each team was given a packet of information including instructions, such as those included at the end of this chapter. (See the Sample Library Mystery Event Rules on page 26.) Since the lights in the library were going to be dimmed, each team also received a flashlight. The introduction can be improvised. Ours went something like this:

> Welcome to the Cushwa-Leighton Library! I am Sheriff Bob Hohl. As you are aware, visiting professor Dr. Ima Gonner is missing. She was last seen in our library on April 1 doing research on the infamous Wild West outlaw Belle Star, an associate of Jesse James. Since the beginning of the month, Dr. Gonner's classes have been cancelled, and her students are very upset about not being able to take her daily pop quizzes on obscure western subjects. At least that's what they *say*.
>
> Our crack security squad has determined that the best hope of finding Professor Gonner is to gather a posse of researchers in an attempt to reconstruct her final hours . . . I'm sorry, I mean her most recent studies here in the library. That's why we've gathered you here tonight. Each team will have to search the library for clues. To begin, you will be issued a packet of information, a regulation flashlight, and an official library pencil. Use your research skills to follow the professor's path and find clues as to her whereabouts. Be sure to keep track of your answers, because they will be vital in finding Professor Gonner. All of the resources the library has to offer are at your disposal. Are you willing to take on this dangerous mission?
>
> Please raise your right hand. [Hands are raised.] Do you solemnly swear to do your best to find Dr. Ima Gonner? Then I hereby deputize you as the official library posse. Remember, Dr. Gonner is depending on you!

At this time, the packets were distributed and the mystery began. Each packet contained a map of the main floor of the library, a pencil, and instructions. Other packets might also include a print copy of the introduction to which the teams can refer. Consider playing the theme from *The Good, the Bad, and the Ugly* on a CD player in the background to set the mood.

Be sure to remind the teams to hang on to their clues and answers as they go along. This will be helpful for them as they work to solve the mysteries. From a practical standpoint, it will make cleaning up after the mystery easier too, since clues and envelopes will be gathered together in one place at the end rather than left throughout the library. (Also, occasionally patrons in academic libraries want to keep their answers as a reference to resources used.)

Let's begin with the initial locations, shown in table 2.2. The Blue and Red teams were instructed that their first clue could be found near the elevator. The Yellow and Green teams were sent to the book drop. The Black and Orange teams went to the photocopier. Once the teams got to these locations, they found envelopes marked with the teams' colors. They were instructed to take the envelope for their team, which contained their first clue. (For illustration, we will follow the Blue Team, whose clues are set out in table 2.3.)

The idea at this point was to send each team to a different location, so the order of the clues in each team's envelopes was different. From the facts we assembled, we wrote clues in the form of questions. On our master copies, we included the answer (in parentheses) and the location where the clue was hidden (this was in italics). This information was deleted from the actual clues, of course. Remember to keep your goals in mind when framing the questions.

To make it easier to position the clues before the event, on the corner or on the back of each envelope, lightly write in pencil the clue number for a specific team and an abbreviation for the location where the clue will be placed—*not* where it leads. The instruction inside the Blue team's packet told them to pick up their first clue at the elevator. We labeled the envelope *Clue 1, Elevator.* Here is how the clue was worded:

CLUE

One of the reference librarians remembers Dr. Gonner asking where to find bound periodicals—specifically, *College and Research Libraries News.* She needed the June 2005 issue.

In volume 66, issue 6, on p. 483, there is an article by George Eberhart. What is Belle's nickname, as given in the subtitle of the article?

Take your next clue, and please put the bound periodical back where it belongs.

As part of our mystery preparation, inside this bound periodical, we had previously placed the labeled envelopes for each team containing the next clue. The bound periodicals at Saint Mary's are located on the lower level of the library, so the Blue team's next clue was *Clue 2, LL.* According to our labeling system, the clue was hidden on the lower level (LL). We had inserted the envelopes for the teams in the June 2005 issue of *College and Research Libraries News* before the mystery began. This was the clue:

CLUE

In her haste, Dr. Gonner accidentally left behind an article about Belle Starr in the ladies' restroom on the second floor.
    According to this article, where was Belle imprisoned?

_____

Take this article to the photocopier on the main floor.

This referenced article was the encyclopedia entry from AllExperts.com. A photocopy of the entry was made for each team, labeled, and put in the ladies' room before the event. This was *Clue 3, 2nd RR*. The clue in the restroom directed the team to the photocopier next.
    Once at the photocopier, the Blue team found another envelope: *Clue 4, Photo:*

CLUE

Obviously Dr. Gonner is interested in anything she can find about Belle Starr. While using Academic Search Premier, she found an article entitled "The Man Who Knew Belle Starr," by Richard Bausch. This article was published in 1987.
    What is the title of the magazine in which this article was published?

_____

Locate this month's copy of this periodical to obtain your next clue.

The answer to this clue was *Atlantic*. Because we had kept the citation and source information together when doing our research, writing the clues was easy. Inside the current issue of *Atlantic* magazine, we had placed the next clue: *Clue 5, Atlantic:*

CLUE

Dr. Gonner used a library book for her research, and she left a bookmark in it. The book is from the Time-Life series "Old West" and is entitled *The Women*. You need to find this book.

In the book, it says, "Belle was the brains behind a gang of _____ thieves in the Oklahoma Territory."

What kind of thieves?

_____

Please return this book to the shelf.

The call number for *The Women* is HQ 1418 .T58. The book contained an envelope with the Blue team's *Clue 6, HQ:*

CLUE

A well-known historian named Glenn Shirley compiled an extensive collection of material on the Wild West. He wrote two books on Belle Starr. One book is entitled *Belle Starr and Her Times: The Literature, the Facts, and the Legends*. Dr. Gonner found a review of this book online in the November 1983 issue of the *Journal of Southern History*.

What is the name of the person who reviewed Shirley's book?

_____

Show this answer to the reference librarian to get your next clue.

One of our goals was to have the teams interact with the staff, so we gave the reference librarian envelopes containing clues. If the team had the correct answer to Clue 6, the librarian gave the team *Clue 7, Ref Lib*, which directed the team to a reference book, where another clue awaited:

CLUE

In order to find out more about Belle Starr, you will need to find Belle's entry in the reference book *Cowboys and the Wild West*.
According to this book, where was Belle born?

_____

Please return this book to the shelf.

The team noted the answer to the question and removed their next clue, *Clue 8, REF:*

CLUE

Dr. Gonner put an item on reserve for her class before she disappeared. It is a written review of the book entitled *Belle Starr: A Novel of the Old West*. The book was reviewed by Sister Avila of the Academy of the Holy Angels.
In what state was Sister Avila living when she wrote this review?

_____

At the reserve desk, the team had to demonstrate that they knew how to request an item on reserve for a particular professor—in this case, Professor Gonner. (We had to be sure that Dr. Gonner was added to our reserve system ahead of time so that the team could locate her item.) Once either they successfully requested the item or the staff member explained the correct procedure to them, the Blue team was given *Clue 9, Reserve:*

CLUE

In WorldCat, there is an article entitled, "At last for the discriminating reader, an unvarnished, straight-shooting, and instructive account of the wild, wild West: containing the irreducible, rock-bottom, and unadorned facts about such desperadoes, sheriffs, gun slingers, cowtown marshals, and assorted riffraff as Wild Bill Hickok, Bat Masterson, Wyatt Earp, Billy the

Kid, and Jesse James; together with various moral lessons and scandalous tales about their fair but frail companions _____ and Belle Starr" by Peter Lyon.
What other female outlaw is named in the article's subtitle?

_____

Once you answer this question, locate the book drop to find your next clue.

Another clue for the Blue team awaited them at the book drop. In fact, all of the locations had an envelope for every team when the mystery started. The clues were picked up in random order, however, so the Blue team had just arrived at the book drop, where the Yellow and Green teams had begun. This is the value of the labeling system: we knew which envelopes to place at each location when we set up the event.

Clue 10, Book drop led the Blue team to another clue:

CLUE

Dr. Gonner was seen watching a video in the audiovisual section. This might be important. The call number of the video is A/V PN 1997 .041.
What is the name of this video?

_____

On the shelf next to the video sat an envelope, *Clue 11, Video*, which contained two pieces of paper: a crossword puzzle (see figure 3.1) and the final instruction.

CLUE

You should have enough clues now to complete this crossword puzzle.
Once you are finished, use the shaded letters to solve the anagram:

_____ _____ _____ _____ _____

This will lead you to the last bit of information you will need to determine Dr. Ima Gonner's whereabouts.

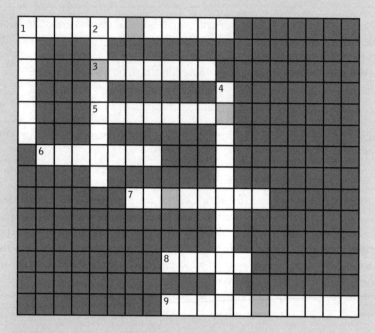

ACROSS

1. Another "fair but frail" outlaw
3. Author of *Belle Starr and Her Times*
5. Video Dr. Gonner watched
6. Where Belle did her prison time
7. Magazine that contains "The Man Who Knew Belle Starr"
8. Man who reviewed Glenn Shirley's book
9. Where reviewer Sister Avila lives

DOWN

1. "Belle was the brains behind a gang of _____ thieves."
2. State where Belle was born
4. Belle's nickname, according to Eberhart

FIGURE 3.1

Belle Starr Mystery Crossword Puzzle

There are a number of online websites with instructions for making your own crossword puzzle, including CrosswordPuzzleGames.com. The answers to the clues the Blue team collected provided the answers to the puzzle. The shaded letters in the puzzle are used to create our anagram.

Figure 3.2 shows the completed puzzle. The answer to the anagram is ATLAS. Do not be surprised if your teams use an online anagram solver to find this final piece of information. We did not anticipate that, but some of the teams tried it and were successful. The answer sheet for each team was in an envelope on the atlas stand, *Clue 12, Atlas:*

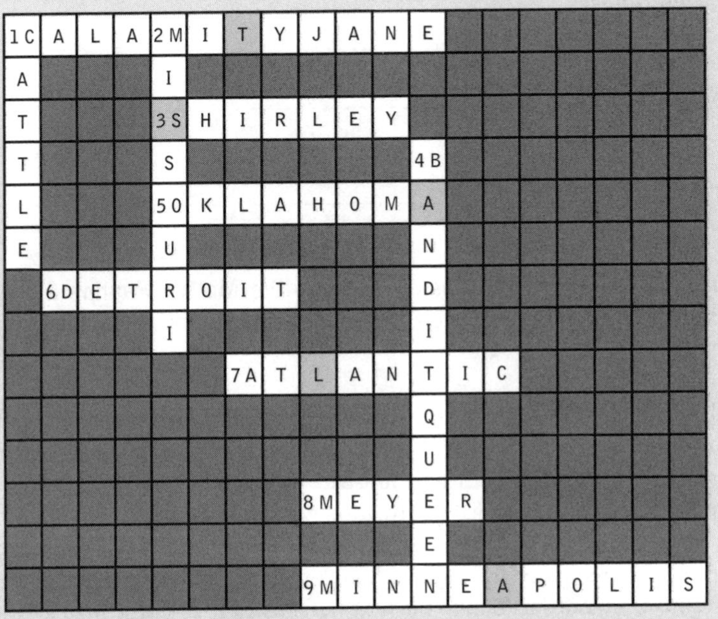

Use the shaded letters to solve this anagram:

_____ _____ _____ _____ _____

Where these items are located, you will find your last clue.

FIGURE 3.2

Belle Starr Mystery Completed Crossword Puzzle and Anagram

CLUE

ANSWER SHEET

A student who works at the circulation desk remembers overhearing Dr. Gonner on her cell phone right before she left the library. The professor said, "After reading this review, I just have to see the Glenn Shirley collection!"

Use the Internet to determine where Dr. Ima Gonner went in order to view the Glenn D. Shirley Western Americana Collection exhibit.

Museum Name: _____

City: _____

State: _____

Bring your team and this answer sheet to the Mother Pauline Seminar Room when you think you know Dr. Gonner's whereabouts! Shhhhhhh . . .

The first team to arrive at the destination with the correct answer was the winner. We had someone posted at that location to record the order in which the teams arrived. Once all teams finished, refreshments were served, prizes were awarded, and additional information was made available.

Our next step was to adapt the clues for the other five teams. The questions for each team remained the same, although the instructions changed to direct the teams from one location to the next (refer to table 2.4). The final location, "Atlas," was the same for all teams.

After we wrote the rest of the team clues, we put the clues in each team's envelope. There were twelve envelopes for each team, each labeled on the corner or the back of the envelope.

Once all of the clues were ready, we sorted them by the labeled location. We needed a set for the elevator, the lower level, the second-floor restroom, the photocopier, *Atlantic* magazine, HQ 1418 .T58, the reference librarian's desk, REF F 586 .C97 1994, the reserve desk, the book drop, the A/V section, and the atlas stand. These sets of clues were placed at each site on the day of the mystery.

We did not need all of the information we found in our research. We used the specific information that was most helpful in achieving our goals. Still, having a variety of facts to choose from is useful. When a mystery is run, we might encounter a problem and determine that a different clue would work better. It is always a good idea to make a specific folder for each mystery and keep information in it for future reference.

Of course, the clues for your library will be different from those we used at Saint Mary's. But combining the resources available to you and the goals you want to achieve for your mystery, you should be able to adapt the Belle Starr script for use in your library.

SAMPLE LIBRARY MYSTERY EVENT RULES

1. The goal of this event is to determine the whereabouts of Dr. Ima Gonner. Clues are hidden throughout the library. The team that first correctly locates Professor Gonner will win prizes.
2. Up to thirty students will participate on a first-come, first-served basis. The participants will be divided into six teams. A sign-up sheet is at the circulation desk. Students may sign up as individuals or as teams. Friends may request to be on the same team, and every effort will be made to accommodate such requests.
3. If space is available at the time of the event, additional students will be admitted.
4. The library will be closed between 10 and 10:30 p.m. for preparations. Students may wait in the vestibule between the glass doors. The front doors will be locked, but not alarmed, during the event. Exit is always possible in case of emergency.
5. Each team will receive a map, a pencil, and a flashlight. The lights in the library will be off or dimmed. Please use caution when moving throughout the building.
6. Teams are to follow the clues for their team's color only. Please do not disturb the clues belonging to the other teams. Reference librarians and helpers will be available to assist the teams.
7. Be sure to hang on to your clues and answers because they will be helpful in solving the mystery.
8. If a clue directs a team to the lower level, please use the elevator. Do not enter Trumper, as other students may be working and the doors to Trumper will be alarmed. Building Services may be working during the event; please be courteous and try to stay out of their way. They have agreed not to vacuum until the event is over.
9. When a team thinks it knows the whereabouts of Dr. Gonner, it should bring the completed answer sheet to the Mother Pauline Room on the second floor. Only one answer sheet per team will be accepted. The first team to arrive with the correct answer will be declared the winner. In the event of a tie, an additional puzzle will be used to determine the winning team.
10. Prizes will be given to the members of the winning team. All students will receive small gifts for participating.
11. Refreshments will be served in the Mother Pauline Room after the event. Please keep food and drinks in this room only.
12. Enjoy!

CHAPTER FOUR

ADAPTATIONS

Obviously you are reading this book because you are interested in planning a mystery event. Let's look at how another library might adapt the script for the Belle Starr mystery to suit its own local collection and facilities.

Clues like those we wrote in chapter 3 consist of two parts: a question and an instruction. Sometimes the question itself leads directly to the next item, in which case the instruction is implied. In other clues, the instruction is specifically stated, as in "take this information to the photocopier" or "show this answer to the reference librarian to get your next clue."

For your mystery, there are likely different locations and resources in your library that you want to stress. In addition to the places mentioned in the Belle Starr mystery, you might want your patrons to use different aspects of your learning commons, stop by your café, find something on microfilm, or delve more deeply into material in a specific discipline. In later chapters, especially chapter 7, which was written for Saint Mary's Psychology Department, you will see more examples of different library resources being used. Basically you should consider including whatever is important—or fun—for your patrons to experience. The predetermined goals of your mystery will help to establish what you want your patrons to experience while they are participating. This is true whether the mystery is a skill review, an orientation, a competition, or a celebratory event.

Be mindful of the manner in which you have patrons move from one location to the next when adapting mysteries and writing your own scripts. Use a grid, even if the mystery is a tour intended for one patron at a time. This organizational tool makes it easier to ensure that your clues flow smoothly from one point to the next; otherwise, things can get confusing pretty quickly. It also helps to mentally or physically walk through the sequence of clues to make sure that they are leading in the right direction.

During the actual mystery, it is possible that patrons will get off course, especially if they answer or interpret a particular clue incorrectly. This is an opportunity, not a disaster, and it is why you have staff members on hand. One popular goal of mystery events is to make your patrons feel more comfortable approaching library staff members. Encourage your patrons to ask for help should they feel lost at any point. In addition, refer to your grid often during the event. By knowing that the patrons have visited a particular location (or not), you can tell whether they are on track. You also can determine their pace and estimate when they will finish.

Obviously it is highly unlikely that your library has the exact same print and online resources as the Cushwa-Leighton Library at Saint Mary's College used for the Belle Starr clues. A library in Oklahoma or one of the other western states is likely to have a lot of information on Belle Starr from which to choose, for example. The remainder of this chapter shows that it is possible for most academic, public, and school libraries to make adaptations of the scripts in this book to suit their own library's collections.

There are a variety of ways to adapt the scripts in this book. One technique is to choose your own theme but use the format of the clues (questions, instructions, puzzles, poems, and others) to write your own script. This means working within the basic framework or composition of the type of mystery you are creating. Another form of adaptation is to stick with the same theme and goals as some of the scripts in this book and then research what material is available at your library on that topic.

Consider what information an average midwestern public library has about Belle Starr. Let's say the St. Joseph County Public Library (SJCPL) in South Bend, Indiana, just down the street from Saint Mary's College, chooses to plan a mystery event to celebrate Women's History Month in March. In that case, they may want to host a mystery built around a Belle Starr theme.

They begin by seeing if they can use any of the clues we already wrote. What portion of the information we noted in chapters 1 and 2 is available at the SJCPL? A few Online Public Access Catalog (OPAC) searches reveal that:

- The SJCPL has the video *Oklahoma!* in its collection.
- The SJCPL owns a copy of *The Women* by the editors of Time-Life Books.
- The full text of one of the articles that we referenced in the *Atlantic* is available in an anthology in the SJCPL fiction collection. "The Man Who Knew Belle Starr" is included in *The Stories of Richard Bausch*, by Richard Bausch.

In addition, the SJCPL has access to the sites we found on the Internet that gave us the following information:

- Belle Starr served six months at the Detroit House of Corrections in Detroit, Michigan, in 1883.
  Source: AllExperts.com encyclopedia entry

- Richard K. Fox wrote *Bella Starr, the Bandit Queen; or, the Female Jesse James* in 1889.
  Source: Infoplease.com entry—www.infoplease.com

- Belle Starr's given name was Myra Belle Shirley.
  Source: Encyclopaedia Britannica entry—www.britannica.com

Now the staff research whether their library has any other resources on Belle Starr that they could use as the basis for new clues. Again, searching online, they find:

- The SJCPL has three books about Belle Starr:

  Belle Starr: A Novel of the Old West, by Deborah Camp (This is the book that Sister Avila in Minneapolis reviewed.)
  Belle Starr, by Carl R. Green and William Sanford
  Belle of the West: The True Story of Belle Starr, by Margaret Rau

- There are other SJCPL nonfiction titles in which they are likely to find more information about Belle Starr, such as:

  True Tales and Amazing Legends of the Old West from *True West* magazine, by the editors of the magazine (Glenn Shirley was published in *True West* magazine.)
  Gangsters, Swindlers, Killers, and Thieves: The Lives and Crimes of Fifty American Villains, edited by Lawrence Block
  What They Didn't Teach You About the Wild West, by Mike Wright
  Women of the Wild West, by Katherine Krohn.

- This library even has two compact disks that include songs about Belle Starr:

  "All the Roadrunning," by Mark Knopfler and Emmylou Harris
  "A Link in the Chain," by Pete Seeger

Apparently there is a lot of information related to Belle Starr available at SJCPL—and that's without considering any online databases to which that library may subscribe. So it appears that using a mixture of existing and new clues to write a mystery script specific to SJCPL should not be a problem. This is actually a bit surprising, given that Belle Starr was a relatively obscure figure in U.S. history until recently.

When you adapt a mystery, you will need to build the framework of it with the information readily available to you. At first glance, you may not think that your library contains enough sources to write your own clues. Do not discount the idea of taking a different tack on your subject matter than we did. The Belle Starr theme, for example, encompasses many avenues to investigate. You might look into resources that explore women in nontraditional occupations or statistics on women who commit crimes. You could inquire into the backgrounds of the outlaws with whom she associated. You might search for information on dime novels, including the impact that Richard Fox's *Bella Starr, the Bandit Queen; or, the Female Jesse James,* published in 1889, had on Belle Starr's legend.

Another possibility is to create the resources you need. Consider making dummy books of actual or fictitious titles. Compose short articles yourself, or print what you can find elsewhere (ever mindful of copyright and fair use issues). Use interlibrary loan to obtain an item that you think will be helpful. If you have extra money in your budget, purchase resources that are consistent with your library's holdings, especially if you believe they will be used again. Perusing other libraries' catalogs and databases will give you an idea of what is available.

Never underestimate the resources you have to work with until you have done your research. If nothing else, you will gain experience and learn something interesting along the way.

Once you know what information exists, review your goals to see what will be most useful. Consider areas of the library that you want your patrons to know more about, such as circulation, interlibrary loan, or even the children's department. Then make up the grid and write the clues. This process can be time-consuming, but if you take it step by step, your script will be effective.

CHAPTER FIVE

NUTS AND BOLTS

Hosting a mystery is similar to other types of events routinely held in a library setting. Nevertheless, certain aspects of mysteries require special attention, especially if you hold the event at night, with the lights dimmed or off. This chapter discusses details to keep in mind when planning a mystery and includes a checklist at the end of the chapter that will help you keep things straight.

The first thing to consider is scheduling. Do you want to hold the mystery at night, with flashlights? If so, do you know how to turn off all of the lights in the library? Will some lights be left on for safety purposes? Will your library be open or closed at the time? If it will be closed, who will be affected? Other members of the library staff? Security? The cleaning crew? Catering? Patrons? Be sure to give all of them plenty of notice in advance. If your library will be open, how will that affect patrons, staff, and those taking part in the mystery? Will a quiet study area be set aside? If the mystery is an orientation tour, it might take place at a set time of the year or with a specific group of patrons. Will this interfere with other library functions? Do you have to reserve your location for the particular date and time? The bottom line is to make sure to notify everyone who needs to know that your event will be taking place; your special arrangements may require someone else to make special arrangements as well.

When you advertise your mystery, make it look compelling. Figure 5.1 shows the advertisement we posted on campus for the Belle Starr Mystery. Remember that patrons who are interested in mysteries tend to be fond of intrigue to begin with. Make announcements through your institution's public relations department. Post fliers and send out e-mails. Make sure to provide information to the individuals who post to your organization's website. Include a notice in your newsletter. Also consider mentioning the mystery while at other library events, or in a classroom setting if you work at a school library. These are all effective ways to communicate with patrons who are interested in library activities.

Once you have chosen a date and time for the mystery, consider having patrons sign up or register. This is helpful so that you know how many to plan

A BeLLe
gone
WILD

Dr. Ima Gonner, a visiting history professor at Saint Mary's this semester, is missing. Dr. Gonner is working on an article about women and crime in the 1880s. The focus of her article is the infamous Belle Starr, a female outlaw from the Wild West.

Search the library after hours for clues
and use your powers of deduction to determine
the whereabouts of Professor Gonner.

Friday, April 13
10:30 p.m.–midnight
Cushwa-Leighton Library

Refreshments will be served. Sign up in the library.
Limit 30 students (individuals/teams welcome)

FIGURE 5.1
Advertisement for the Belle Starr Mystery

for and when you have reached your participation limit. Take into account whether patrons will be registering as individuals or as teams. Can individual patrons who sign up be combined to make up a team? Who is in charge of keeping track of the registrations? Be sure to give this person a sign-up sheet to record not only the names of the patrons who will be attending but also their contact information.

When patrons register, you may want to give them a flier or send them a postcard, e-mail, or text message as a reminder. If you think it is necessary, you can print out rules or procedures for the event that might include the location in the library where the patrons should report, what will happen if someone arrives late, or whether there are any specific areas of the library that you would like patrons to avoid. A sample is included at the end of chapter 3. Also, let the participants know whether you want them to wear a particular color or a costume to heighten their involvement in the mystery. Encourage your staff to get in the spirit and wear the proper attire too.

Make sure you will have enough staff members on hand to run the mystery. This includes a reference librarian and a circulation staff member, especially if any of the clues require the patrons to "check out" material. Other staff members might be needed in areas such as the information desk, the reserve desk, or the A/V area, depending on the layout of your facility and what your mystery entails.

You might want to post staff members in your print collection, near books that are mentioned in the clues. These assistants can help the patrons if necessary and keep an eye out to be sure that the materials are reshelved in their proper place, with all remaining clues intact. (Through experience, we have found that patrons under age 18 are more likely to consider tampering with clues to get an advantage than are older patrons.) If you will be serving refreshments at the event, be sure to mention that in your advertising. If your library's policies do not normally allow food and beverages in the building, perhaps you can arrange for an exception in a designated area. Serving snacks seems to encourage patron participation, especially among college and university students. The refreshments could be the standard cookies, chips, and fruit punch, or you might offer something more in keeping with your theme, such as trail mix, beef jerky, cactus cookies, and virgin margaritas for a Belle Starr mystery. It would be fun to serve chocolate frogs and Bernie Bott's Every Flavor Beans for a Harry Potter–type mystery. For recipes for nonalcoholic Butterbeer, go to mugglenet.com. If you are in an academic library at a college that uses an independent food service company, be sure to give enough notice of the event, especially if it is after-hours. You might be surprised how far the supplier is willing to go to help you.

Bring in props and decorations to enhance the atmosphere. Most of the time, appropriate items can be borrowed from coworkers. A few of the photographs in this book show displays and costumes used at Saint Mary's. Not only does the decor set a congenial tone for the mystery, but it improves the approachability of the library staff in the eyes of the patrons. A little imagination and raiding closets and attics can keep costs to a minimum.

Do not underestimate the value of visual and sound effects: a chalk outline, footprints, a door slamming, a scream. All sorts of special effects can be employed to create an entertaining atmosphere for your event. Your patrons will appreciate that you put in the extra effort. It will make hosting the mystery more fun for you and your staff too.

Another nice touch is to include gifts for your participants. These do not have to be elaborate. They might be related to the theme of the event or be standard public relations items for your library. At a school event, it might involve extra credit points. If your mystery is a competition, present prizes to

```
G  J  K  L  S  W  N  O  R  E  F  M  C  R  T
F  Z  X  N  V  V  Q  E  M  H  L  E  K  Q  M
T  K  R  H  S  Y  N  M  L  B  L  Q  G  F  V
P  N  O  H  A  N  R  I  C  M  A  J  B  G  U
A  C  S  J  O  D  H  B  T  R  B  X  Y  Y  V
A  N  S  G  R  M  Q  I  M  H  O  L  R  L  I
W  L  E  I  J  W  G  P  O  L  N  F  X  Z  J
R  T  F  E  Y  Q  V  I  T  V  W  S  E  Y  K
J  O  O  G  U  X  D  V  H  Y  Q  R  V  I  V
Q  Q  R  W  I  V  H  F  O  U  N  D  N  W  C
Z  G  P  Q  Z  Y  U  Y  R  K  D  A  K  L  O
I  A  I  W  S  V  Z  W  I  R  U  W  H  D  P
X  X  I  A  T  D  P  X  N  B  O  B  E  Y  N
J  R  I  C  A  B  H  V  Z  Z  J  M  V  I  C
H  R  F  K  N  N  F  Z  I  T  T  U  U  X  X
```

Circle the following words in the puzzle:

FOUND PROFESSOR GONNER

FIGURE 5.2

Mystery Tiebreaker for the Belle Star Mystery

the individuals or teams that do well. A certificate of completion works nicely for an orientation tour. We gave every student at the Belle Starr mystery small squirt guns when the event was over, and they loved them! Ordering items through a party supply company or wholesale distributor is inexpensive. Again, remember to place your order far enough in advance. Dollar stores can be good sources of gifts and prizes too, including flashlights. Look for packages of flashlights that include batteries to save money. It is a good idea to label the flashlights and collect them right after the event so that they can be used again.

Two additional things that you might want to have ready are something to fill time and a tiebreaker. Patrons work through the mystery at different speeds, so some will finish ahead of others, and you may have stragglers. Be sure to have books on hand related to your theme or even a PowerPoint presentation to have running in the background. These measures can be informative and perhaps even entertaining, and they will keep your patrons busy while they are waiting for everyone to finish.

If your mystery is a competition, prepare for a possible tie. If two individuals or teams finish simultaneously, be ready with multiple prizes, or use some sort of a tiebreaker. We have designed a word search puzzle for each mystery just in case. These can be made online at a site such as puzzlemaker.discoveryeducation.com. So far, we have not had to use a tiebreaker, but having one available does provide peace of mind. Figure 5.2 shows the tiebreaker for the Belle Starr mystery.

Once all of your preparations are done and the day of the event arrives, place the sets of clues in their designated locations. If the clues are unlikely to be disturbed, you can place them early in the day. Clues at the photocopiers, reference desk, or circulation should be set out right before the event begins. Have your packets prepared, staff in place, and the person who will be giving your introduction standing by. Bring your camera to take pictures for your newsletter. Then watch with pride as your patrons excitedly use the library, racing—often running—as they look for their clues. Congratulate yourself on a job well done!

MYSTERY EVENT CHECKLIST

❑ Sign-up sheet/registration information

❑ Helpers needed:

    Reference librarian   Circulation staff member
    Reserve desk   A/V section
    Call # locations   Final destination (timer)

    _____   _____

    _____   _____

❑ Place clues:

    _____   _____   _____

    _____   _____   _____

    _____   _____   _____

    _____   _____   _____

❑ Notify:

    Security department   Cleaning crew
    Food services   Public relations

❑ Advertising

    Fliers   Newsletter
    Library website   External website

❑ Find out how and where to control lights

❑ Supplies

    Envelopes   Props
    Flashlights   Batteries
    Maps   Pencils

❑ Introduction (and introducer) ready

❑ Costumes

❑ Special effects

❑ Refreshments

    _____   _____

❑ Prizes

❑ Participation gifts or certificates

❑ Tiebreaker

❑ Time filler

❑ Other _____

PART TWO

SAMPLE SCRIPTS

The chapters in part 2 comprise scripts that can be easily adapted to various library settings. Each chapter presents a different type of mystery and instructions about how the mystery can be run. Refer to the chapters in part 1 should you have any questions regarding the design of your own mystery

CHAPTER SIX

ORIENTATION TOUR SCRIPT

STOLEN PAINTINGS MYSTERY

This mystery is a self-guided orientation to the library. In this example, we again use the St. Joseph County Public Library in South Bend, Indiana. The premise is that five paintings created by local artists and displayed in the main branch of the library were allegedly stolen. The patrons' job is to determine who stole the paintings. The script is written so that the same clues can be used over and over again by different patrons. It is also possible for this tour to be self-guided by a group of patrons or led by a staff member.

In this example, the mystery begins at the return desk, which is to the right of the main entrance. (Table 6.1 shows the grid for this mystery.) New patrons might be given the introduction to the library self-guided tour when they apply for a library card, for instance. You may want to find a place to display each of the clues in the location or department with which it is associated. If that is done, some type of symbol—such as a question mark or magnifying glass—should be identified with the clue. This will help to catch the patrons' attention and lead them to the next location.

Choose the areas that you want patrons to visit. Your goals might be providing a layout of the facility, an overview of services, a chance to meet the librarians and staff, or examples of policies and procedures. The key is to provide some familiarity with the layout and services of the library so that patrons know what is available. Be sure to make other staff members aware of the tour so that they can assist any patrons who might need help.

In this example, a map of the library is made available to patrons. The clues direct patrons to different departments and give a brief explanation of what the department does. There is one call number reference, but feel free to add more. Also, you may want to include a clue that involves an Internet search; this tour does not contain that element.

The last clue mentions a reward when the mystery is solved. This is an ideal opportunity to give out promotional materials for the library or certificates of completion. Or perhaps the reward can be receiving one's library card at the end rather than in the beginning. As usual, decide what is best for you and your library, and don't be afraid to experiment.

Some passages in the script that follows are explanations directed to you. These are all italicized.

Library Self-Guided Tour

Thank you for being here today. We really need your help! As you probably heard, five paintings created by local artists and displayed in the main branch of the library since 1994 were stolen. The thief no doubt planned to hold them for a large ransom. You, our stellar detective, are our only hope to determine the identity of the thief and claim the reward.

TABLE 6.1
Grid for the Stolen Paintings Script

Location of Clue	Leads to
Return Desk	Reference & Information
Reference & Information	Kids' Place
Kids' Place	Sights & Sounds
Sights & Sounds	Local History & Genealogy
Local History & Genealogy	1st floor restrooms
1st floor restrooms	Reference collection
Reference collection	OPAC
OPAC	News, Magazines, & Fiction
News, Magazines, & Fiction	Lower level
Lower level	Facility Manager's Office
Facility Manager's Office	Publicity Office

So let's get straight to it. Here are the facts as we know them. When the library director, Dr. Napoleon, arrived at work last Wednesday, the back door to the building was propped open. After a quick look around, he determined that certain paintings were missing:

Six P.M., by David Allen
Castle Garden, by Linda Freel
Entrance to Storytime Room, by Kim Hoffmann
Learning the Letter B, by Alan Larkin
Knowledge, by William Tourtillotte

The paintings have been recovered and are hung in their proper places again. But we still do not know the identity of the thief. Can you help us?

For some reason, the thief left notes around the library. By following the trail of notes, we hope you will figure out the person's identity. Feel free to ask questions of any staff at any time. And be sure to look for this icon *[insert the icon that you are using here]* to indicate the presence of a note or clue.

In order to determine the identity of the thief, you may need access to library materials. Since you are at the return desk, apply for a library card. If you already have a card, you may begin to try to solve the mystery right away.

Proceed to the reference and information desk on the first floor of the library.

Ask the reference librarian for a map of the library. It contains a separate page for each floor. At the reference and information desk, you will see a copy of the first clue the thief left behind. Remember to keep track of your answers.

CLUE 1

The first note left by the thief tells something about what the Reference and Information Department does:

reference librarians have lots of the Knowledge. they answer questions and provide all kinds of Information. help is always reaDy. just aSk.

Isn't it strange how some letters are lowercase and others are capitals? What do the capital letters spell?

_____ _____ _____ _____

Go to the department that caters to these particular patrons, and you will find another note.

CLUE 2

The name of the Children's Services department is the Kids' Place. You can see that it is very colorful and welcoming. Since three of the paintings that were stolen are from this area, obviously the thief had been here before . . . perhaps many times with his or her own children?

Again, a note was left behind:

There's fun in this room, but learning, too. So much to do, and computers for you.

This time it seems that the underlined letters must mean something. Can you unscramble them to make a word?

_____ _____ _____ _____ _____

If you go to the department where you can find this type of material shelved, you will find the next clue.

CLUE 3

What is the name of this audiovisual area? _____

Perhaps the thief is a big music fan or movie buff. In any case, the thief thinks he or she is sooooo clever. Here's a poem the thief left for us to decipher:

Imagine checking out music, videos, and dvds for free.
Libraries give us so much to see.
Do you know where to research your family tree?
It's as easy as efg.

7	5	14	5	1	12	15	7	25

Use the code below to discover another department in the library where the thief placed a clue.

1 = a, 2 = b, 3 = c, 4 = d, 5 = e, 6 = f, 7 = g, 8 = h, 9 = i, 10 = j, 11 = k, 12 = l, 13 = m, 14 = n, 15 = o, 16 = p, 17 = q, 18 = r, 19 = s, 20 = t, 21 = u, 22 = v, 23 = w, 24 = x, 25 = y, 26 = z

CLUE 4

Is it time for a break? Maybe not, but you'd better go by the restrooms on the first floor, because we found a note near there too.

You would be right to conclude that the law is important
in a crime like this. If you catch me, you are probably going
to want to throw the book at me. I'd suggest the book with
the call number 340.03 B561b.

Look for this book in the reference section on the main floor. If you need help finding it, do not hesitate to ask a reference librarian.

What is the title of this book? _____

Since you are near some public access computers, look for any note the thief might have placed in that area.

(Note that some public access computers can be used only to search the library's online catalog. On other public access computers, you can use the Internet, check out a social networking website, or read your e-mail.)

CLUE 5

Sure enough, the thief did leave a clue here. He or she is very cunning and thinks we'll be fooled by another puzzle. Can you find a library word within these scrambled letters?

A	K	D	J	O	D	L	E
C	J	F	B	N	H	K	D
J	N	I	T	G	U	R	E
I	E	C	S	K	I	L	X
X	G	T	P	J	O	M	H
V	K	I	W	U	Q	T	R
I	U	O	Q	S	I	L	O
K	Z	N	D	Z	U	S	E
L	I	E	K	P	J	M	F

The word is _____.

This is the name of the section that encompasses material created by the imagination that is not factual. It is full of books to read for fun and includes mysteries, romantic novels, westerns, and fantasy stories. This section is located on the second floor.

Ask a librarian or staff member for the telephone number of this department.

Near this same area, you will see the library's collection of newspapers and magazines. Once again, the thief left another clue behind. Can you find it?

CLUE 6

This note is a bit cryptic, don't you think?

> **My crime is all over the news, I see. It is so funny to be reading about me. But if the library were to go away, that indeed would be a sad, sad day. No books to read. No games to play. No learning for you. No pay for me.**

Hmmm. The thief must be someone on the payroll. Sounds like an inside job. But there are a lot of employees. Who could it be?

The clues have led us all over the library. Was there something the thief wants you to see? Or, better yet, is there some place you have not seen at all?

If you look at your map, is there an obvious location where you have not been? What about the lower level? That is where the auditorium and public meeting rooms are located.

Take the elevator down there to make sure you are not missing something.

CLUE 7

The note left in this area is a riddle:

> **<u>Knowledge</u> is a wonderful thing to have. Imagine the <u>entrance to the storytime room</u> at about <u>6 p.m.</u> Or a child, sitting in a <u>castle garden, learning the letter B.</u> None of this would be known, would it, if it were not for me?**

This time the thief made reference to all of the paintings that were stolen, and underlined their titles. You must be on the right track.

From the sounds of the last line of the clue, the thief sounds like someone who does a lot to make the library popular. You are so close to determining the thief's identity. Walk around and see if there are any clues around here.

Look, there! On the facility manager's door . . .

CLUE 8

It looks as if you've come to the end. This is the last clue:

Serr choyvpvgl sbe gur yvoenel!

Use this code to decipher the message:

a = n, b = o, c = p, d = q, e = r, f = s, g = t, h = u, i = v, j = w, k = x, l = y, m = z

"Choyvpvgl?" Is there someone in charge of that? There is an entire office for that here on the lower level. Looks like the thief was Ny Fubjzna, who is in charge of Choyvpvgl Services.

Using the code, Ny Fubjzna = _____

Good job! You did it!

Now that you have had a comprehensive tour of the library, you should be able to find whatever you need, or at least know where to ask about it.

Go back up to the return desk on the first floor and tell them who stole the paintings to claim your reward!

Answer Key

1. Kids
2. Music
3. Sights and Sounds Department; genealogy
4. *Black's Law Dictionary*
5. Fiction; 574-282-4614
8. Free publicity for the library! Al Showman

CHAPTER SEVEN

DISCIPLINE-SPECIFIC SCRIPT

PSYCHOLOGY/

SALEM WITCH TRIALS MYSTERY

It is often helpful, particularly in an academic or school setting, to offer a mystery that incorporates resources specific to a particular discipline. At Saint Mary's College, all seniors must complete a comprehensive project in their major subject. In psychology, the seniors in the seminar course conduct either a literature review or a research study.

The rationale behind a discipline-specific script is to present resources in one subject. This script was developed with a psychology professor to determine what materials and skills she believed would be most helpful for senior seminar students to review in the first week or two of class. Consequently the goals involve very specific aptitudes, reference works, and databases:

- Locate the *APA Publication Manual* and use proper APA format in a reference.
- Locate the current *Diagnostic and Statistical Manual of Mental Disorders* (DSM) to answer questions about particular disorder.
- Use PsycARTICLES to find a full-text article.
- Use PsycINFO to conduct a search and narrow it by delimiters.
- Locate a bound journal.
- Retrieve a book given only the call number.
- Find specific information in a past comprehensive paper on reserve.
- Locate proper citation format from an online APA-style resource.
- Use two sources to illustrate how to properly format headings in APA style.
- Find the author of a relevant book using WorldCat.
- Use interlibrary loan to request an item.
- Find medical reference information.

Three psychology professors were in the library with their classes when the mystery was conducted. So were staff members and helpers, some dressed in period garb.

The theme of this mystery is the witch trials in Salem, Massachusetts, in the 1690s. The students work as individuals or in groups of two to three, so the grid includes many more columns. (Table 7.1 shows the team names at the top and the order in which they are given the clues. If you have studied the witch trials, these names may sound familiar to you: they are the names of some of the alleged witches who were hanged.) The clues ask questions about a variety of resources within the library, but for this mystery, the instructions are always the same: once the students believe they have correctly answered the question, they show their answer to their professor, who must approve it (e.g., correct citation format using APA style). If the answer is acceptable, the students are given their next clue. If not, their professor or a reference librarian helps them find the correct one. (Each professor and librarian is given a set of clues with the correct answers to use as a key.)

TABLE 7.1
Grid for the Psychology/Salem Witch Trials Script

Bishop	Nurse	Good	Martin	Howe	Burroughs	Proctor	Corey	Parker	Wildes
1	10	11	9	4	7	5	13	3	12
2	1	6	7	5	8	12	9	13	4
3	12	10	8	7	13	1	4	2	11
4	8	7	10	11	9	3	5	6	2
5	13	8	2	12	1	6	3	11	9
6	3	4	12	2	10	7	1	9	5
7	9	3	4	1	2	11	12	1	13
8	5	12	13	6	11	9	10	7	3
9	6	5	11	8	4	13	2	10	7
10	7	1	5	9	3	8	6	4	10
11	2	13	1	3	6	4	7	12	8
12	4	2	3	13	5	10	11	8	6
13	11	9	6	10	12	2	8	5	1
14	14	14	14	14	14	14	14	14	14

Once the teams complete their clues, the students and professors meet in a conference room or in their classroom to discuss the nature of the mystery. Rather than being a "whodunit," the students are asked to review and discuss the information they collected to determine a possible diagnosis for the children who appeared "possessed" by witchcraft.

The professors and librarians must agree in advance whether the mystery will take place during class time, outside class time, or even when the library is closed. In addition, the professors need to decide whether the mystery will be mandatory for their students or for extra credit. Finally, a brief questionnaire is included that can be given to students after they complete the mystery—and again after they finish their comprehensive paper—to determine the effectiveness of the mystery as a review or teaching tool. (The questionnaire is provided at the end of the chapter.)

This style of mystery could be adapted for a school library, most likely with fewer clues. Within a public library, the participants should share a common interest for a discipline-specific script to be most effective. It also might be used in a special library as an orientation to the range of resources available. The resources used and level of difficulty should be adjusted for the age and knowledge level of the patrons. The introduction, which follows, was given to the students in class, ahead of the mystery.

Some passages in the script that follows are explanations directed to you. These are all italicized.

Introduction

Salem Witch Trials:
A Library Mystery for Psychology Senior Seminar

Sally Studious is a psychology major. She worked all summer and did some traveling, but that didn't keep her from worrying about her senior comprehensive paper. She has a few ideas for topics that she wants to check out. She also wants to make sure that she is familiar with the library and the resources it has to offer before she gets too far into her senior seminar course.

During her junior year, Sally read the play *The Crucible* by Arthur Miller in her English class. She was moved by the recounting of the Salem witch trials of 1692 in which fourteen women and six men were convicted of practicing witchcraft and hanged after a group of children accused them of being witches.

In this mystery, you will follow the path of Sally Studious as she researches various aspects of the Salem witch trials for her paper. After answering each question or completing each task, show your work to your professor. If you have correctly completed the task, your professor will provide you with the next clue.

Prizes will be awarded to the teams that complete this first and most accurately. Everyone who participates will receive extra credit points.

Here are some suggestions that may help you solve the mystery:

- Report to the library at 10 p.m. on September 7. The building will be dark, but flashlights will be provided.
- Bring a copy of the *APA Publication Manual,* although the library does have a copy on reserve.
- Work as a team of two or three (see the sign-up sheet).
- Work quickly . . . running is allowed!
- Remember that it is just as important to be accurate as to be fast.
- Be prepared for ghostly sightings.
- Make use of library resources to the best of your ability.
- As always, the reference librarian will be available to answer any questions you may have.

- Hang on to your clues, because they will be helpful in the end . . .
- Have fun!

Retrace Sally's steps in the library, and see if your team can be the first to successfully and accurately complete the tasks, and take a stab at explaining what caused the events in Salem in 1692 to get so out of hand.

—

Number the clues to help with the grid and the answer key. Put each teams' clues in order according to the grid before the mystery begins.

CLUE 1

Team: _____

Sally is interested in better understanding the validity of the eyewitness testimony of young children in order to determine how trustworthy the Salem children were as trial witnesses.

a. Using PsycINFO, Sally has located a book, *Jeopardy in the Courtroom: A Scientific Analysis of Children's Testimony.* Find and print the detailed citation and abstract for this chapter.

b. Using the *APA Publication Manual,* find the section on reference list examples. What is the example given of the reference to a journal article with three to six authors? Underline any portions that are italicized.

_____

_____

_____

c. Write how Sally should reference the book *Jeopardy in the Courtroom* using APA format at the end of her paper. Underline any portions that are italicized.

_____

_____

_____

Show these findings to your professor to get your next clue.

CLUE 2

Team: _____

Sally would like to find an article in PsycINFO about the credibility of child witnesses.

a. Conduct a search to find a chapter in a book published in 1990 that discusses factors that may influence children's susceptibility to false eyewitness testimony, including within the sociocultural context of the Salem witch trials. When you find this chapter, print the detailed citation and abstract for it.

b. List at least four subjects/delimiters or keywords that Sally could use to begin and narrow her search on this topic.

_____   _____

_____   _____

_____   _____

Show these findings to your professor to get your next clue.

CLUE 3

Team: _____

Sally is excited when she learns from the reference librarian that she can always find the full text of articles using PsycARTICLES. She is interested in the confessions made by those accused of witchcraft. In PsycARTICLES she finds a critical analysis that looks at psychological explanations for witch confessions.

a. Print the full text of the PDF of this article on both sides of paper.

b. Within this article, Sally found fascinating information about confessions and suggestibility. Locate the direct quote she found from a group of accused Salem witches. Mark the quote to identify it.

c.   What are the names of the six accused witches to whom this state-
     ment is attributed? (Hint: The answer can be found within the
     library's print collection.)

_____   _____

_____   _____

_____   _____

d.   What would Sally cite as the source for these names in her
     references?

_____

_____

_____

Show these findings to your professor to get your next clue.

CLUE 4

Team: _____

Sally wants to get practice using the library's databases. She decides to
try Academic Search Premier.

a.   Find an article by David Harley that looks at the state of witchcraft in
     Salem, Massachusetts, and discusses the diagnosis of possession.

b.   Write down the quote in the article attributed to Edwin Powers in
     1966 on p. 307.

_____

_____

_____

Show these findings to your professor to get your next clue.

CLUE 5

Team: _____

Sally is intrigued by the concepts of mass hysteria and social delusions after reading about the witch trials. She'd like to find more information.

a.   Use WorldCat to find the closest library that owns the book *Little Green Men, Meowing Nuns and the Head-Hunting Panics* published in 2001. What is the location of that library?

_____

b.   What is the call number of that book?

_____

c.   Who is the author of that book?

_____

Show these findings to your professor to get your next clue.

CLUE 6

Team: _____

Sally discovers that the mass hysteria exhibited in Salem is a form of collective behavior. She wonders if we have a book here in our library about collective behavior.

a.   Use the Cushwa-Leighton Library online catalog to find the book Sally used that was published in 1991.

What is the title of the book?

_____

What is the call number of the book?

_____

b.   On what page of this book can you find a table detailing McPhail's examination of elementary forms of collective behavior?

_____

c.   According to the table, wailing is a form of collective _____.

Return this book to its proper location on the shelf. Show these findings to your professor to get your next clue.

CLUE 7

Team: _____

Sally is surprised to read that Betty Parris and Abigail Williams were often the only witnesses testifying against an accused witch. She wants to know if this is common, given the age of the girls and the seriousness of the accusations.

a.   In PsycINFO, she does a search on the term *witnesses*. She is overwhelmed by the number of results she gets. How many results were generated?

_____

b.   She decides to narrow the search by the subject "legal testimony" because the girls were speaking at trial. How many results were generated by narrowing the search?

_____

c.   Narrowing the search by which subject listed would give Sally the fewest results?

_____

d.   How many results does the search in part c generate?

_____

Show these findings to your professor to get your next clue.

CLUE 8

Team: _____

Sally is trying to find answers to questions about how to format her paper. The reference librarian points out that Sally can find this information under "Research Help" on the library's web page. This information includes links to online style manuals.

a. List two of the three helpful URLs/links given on the library's website on how to cite resources in APA style.

_____

_____

b. Find the American Psychological Association home page online.

What is the URL?

_____

Using the link to APA Style, locate the Frequently Asked Questions. What is the first FAQ?

_____

_____

_____

_____

Show these findings to your professor to get your next clue.

CLUE 9

Team: _____

Sally has located an interesting chapter in the book *Demonophobia*, by Boris Sidis, in PsycINFO, but our library does not own the book.

a.   Print the detailed citation and abstract.

b.   From within PsycINFO, use the FindText feature to request the item through interlibrary loan (ILL). Fill out the form, and *before* you send it to ILL, print a copy of your book request for your records.

c.   Ask the reference librarian where you can get the photocopy of this chapter once it has arrived.

_____

Show these findings to your professor to get your next clue.

CLUE 10

Team: _____

Sally is pretty confident about her ability to do the research necessary for her paper. But in order to get a better idea of what is required, she would like to take a look at a successful senior comprehensive that was done in the past.

a.   Ask at the reserve desk to see a copy of a senior comprehensive placed on reserve under your professor's name.

What is the name of the student who wrote this?

_____

What is the running head for this comp?

_____

Using the *APA Publication Manual,* find out the maximum length allowed for a running head.

_____

b. Use the *APA Publication Manual* to find the function of *headings*. Write one of the functions of headings below.

_____

_____

c. The *APA Publication Manual* has an entire chapter on manuscript preparation that is very helpful. Find the manuscript preparation page in the *APA Publication Manual* that explains how to format three levels of headings for a journal article. Make a photocopy of this page.

Show these findings to your professor to get your next clue.

CLUE 11

Team: _____

While researching information on collective behavior and mass hysteria, Sally begins to see similarities between what happened in Salem in the 1600s and more recent events. She looks for an example to support her reasoning.

a. Find the original article on mass psychogenic illness at a Tennessee high school (Jones et al., 2000). Print the detailed citation and abstract.

b. Use FindText to see if our library has the article and, if so, where it is located.

c. Make a photocopy of the periodical article, reducing it if necessary so that you can fit two pages on one sheet of paper at a time, side-by-side (*not* double-sided).

Show these findings to your professor to get your next clue.

CLUE 12

Team: _____

Sally is still curious about what caused Betty Parris and Abigail Williams to behave so strangely.

a. She read about one modern theory that the girls ate rye containing a fungus, ergot, with hallucinogenic properties. Use the *Diagnostic and Statistical Manual of Mental Disorders,* 4th ed. (DSM-IV) to find the diagnostic code for Other or Unknown Substance-Induced Delirium. Make a photocopy of this page.

_____

b. Locate an article about the ergot theory as it pertains to Salem. Print the detailed citation and abstract.

c. Using the DSM-IV, find the diagnostic criteria for code 300.11. Make a photocopy of this page.

What is the name of this disorder?

_____

Return the DSM-IV to its proper location in the library. Show these findings to your professor to get your next clue.

CLUE 13

Team: _____

Sally heard a theory that Betty Parris and Abigail Williams acted strangely because they suffered from Arctic hysteria, also known as winter madness. One of the causes of Arctic hysteria is hypocalcemia.

a. Define hypocalcemia.

_____

b. What was your source for this definition?

_____

c. Sally wants to know if there is research on a connection between hysteria and hypocalcemia. She asks the reference librarian for a good source for medical information like this. The reference librarian suggests the periodical index MEDLINE. Write the title of the article by C. H. Snyder that Sally finds. Print the detailed citation and abstract for your reference.

_____

_____

Show these findings to your professor to get your next clue.

CLUE 14

Team: _____

Examine the information you have collected about the behaviors observed in the "possessed" girls and the possible causes of these behaviors. Is the girls' behavior consistent with the diagnosis for Other or Unknown Substance-Induced Delirium? Is it consistent with Conversion Disorder? With Arctic madness? Be prepared to explain your reasoning and cite sources.

When you are ready, go to the Mother Pauline Room on the second floor to provide your assessment of whether the girls could be diagnosed with Other or Unknown Substance-Induced Delirium, with Conversion Disorder, with Artic madness, or with none of these diagnoses.

Answer Key

1. *Jeopardy in the Courtroom*—PsycINFO, *APA Manual*
2. Suggestibility of preschoolers' recollections—PsycINFO, delimiters
3. Witchcraft in the histories of psychiatry—PsycARTICLES, BF 1573 .A2 B96 2002
4. "Explaining Salem: Calvinist psychology"... (quote)—Academic Search Premier
5. *Little Green Men*—WorldCat
6. *Myth of the Madding Crowd*—OPAC, HM 281 .M37
7. Narrow "witnesses" search—PsycINFO
8. Library web page, APA web page—APA style
9. *Demonophobia*—PsycINFO, FindText, interlibrary loan
10. Sample comps—*APA Manual*
11. Mass psychogenic illness—PsycINFO, FindText, bound periodical
12. Substance-Induced Delirium and Conversion Disorder—DSM-IV
13. Arctic hysteria—Google, MEDLINE
14. Diagnosis—Mother Pauline Room

POST-MYSTERY QUESTIONNAIRE

Please take a moment to answer the following questions:

1. Did you enjoy the mystery? ❏ Yes ❏ No

2. How long did it take you to complete the mystery?

   _____

3. Is there additional information that should have been included?

   _____

   _____

   _____

4. Were there any questions that were too difficult or not helpful at all?

   _____

   _____

   _____

5. Do you think the mystery will be/was worthwhile as a review for writing your own senior comprehensive paper? Why or why not?

   _____

   _____

   _____

6. Would this type of exercise be helpful in another one of your classes? If so, which one(s)?

   _____

   _____

Thank you!

CHAPTER EIGHT

CHARACTER-DRIVEN SCRIPT

UNFRIENDLY FRIENDS MYSTERY

This script is for lovers of the mystery dinner format. The theme of the mystery is a banquet where members of the Friends of the Library are to present donations and potentially receive a special award for their philanthropic efforts. The incentive for the mystery might be to celebrate a milestone, offer a fun alternative to a book club meeting, promote the library to a specific audience, put a twist on a retirement party, or host an event related to a topic of interest to the participants.

The mystery dinner format traditionally does not put any emphasis on using library resources. Rather, it focuses on characters who are portrayed by staff or volunteers. These characters are knowledgeable about the plot from the beginning so they can play their role to the fullest. The characters will know whodunit; the audience will have to solve the crime given the information that the characters pass along. In fact, these types of events usually are not held in libraries but rather in restaurants or banquet halls. In devising a plot, we suggest hosting the event in the library so that its facilities or acquisitions can be featured. Decide whether the patrons will be seated at tables or mingling in a defined area. It is important that the patrons remain close together to see and hear the action.

Typically there are a half-dozen or so characters, all of them suspects. The crime is usually a murder, as it is in this example. All of the characters have a motive. It is helpful if one character serves as a detective/inspector or moderator for the event. This person could be a suspect as well, but mainly helps to walk the audience through the clues so that the mystery flows. Be sure to create interesting characters whose interaction with one another, as well as with the audience, will provide good theater. Typically one of the characters will have to die—unless the death precedes the start of the event and is discussed in the past tense.

For this mystery, make a list of characters and motives, as well as a timetable of events. The characters need to be role playing throughout, up to the time that one of them is accused or forced to confess. (Since they all have a motive, it is possible to host the mystery multiple times, each time with a different ending.) The characters are free to move about and should socialize with the audience, answering questions and giving the patrons a stake in the outcome of the mystery. It is a good idea to have a dress rehearsal so the characters have an idea of what to say, where the action will take place, and how they will interact with one another.

Be sure to stick closely to your timetable. The characters are free to ad lib, but must make their motives clear to the audience. Be sure to stagger the activities involving the characters so that everyone in the audience hears and sees everything. You don't want them to miss any clues. For this type of mystery, clues might include spoken words, notes, and incriminating physical evidence.

Each audience member should be given a program that appears to outline the evening's activities (see figure 8.1). It should include the names of the

You are cordially invited to the

Lazy River Chamber of Commerce 2008 Philanthropy Awards

Lazy River Public Library
December 1, 2008
7 p.m. –9 p.m.

Welcome: Mr. Reed A. Lot, Director,
Lazy River Public Library

Reception: open bar and hors d'oeuvres

AWARD FINALISTS

First National Bank
To date, the bank has donated $25,000 to the
Needy Children's Fund and $15,000 to the Food Bank

Modest Foundation
To date, the Modest Foundation has given
over $100,000 to 18 Lazy River charities

Rich Family Trust
To date, the Rich Family Trust has made
over $100,000 in donations to fund medical research
and literacy programs

Presentation of the Award: Mayor I. M. Pompous

Special Thanks to the
Friends of the Lazy River Public Library:

MRS. PRUDENCE MODEST   MR. COY N. MODEST   MS. DEE KUP
MRS. VI L. RICH   MR. PHIL T. RICH   MR. IRA RICH

FIGURE 8.1
Mock Program for the Unfriendly Friends Mystery

characters for their reference. They should also be given an answer sheet and a pen or pencil so that they can take notes if they like. (An answer sheet is provided on page 74.)

The detective/investigator character is in charge of keeping the mystery flowing and on pace. He or she should have access to a clock and the grids. Once the killer is named, it is the detective/investigator who will take the killer into custody.

Audience members can receive prizes or certificates. They should have an opportunity to mingle with the characters afterward.

This mystery has alternate endings. The audience can choose the killer, or the identity can be predetermined.

Some passages in the script that follows are explanations directed to you. These are all italicized.

Summary

The Friends of the Lazy River Public Library are in attendance at a banquet honoring philanthropists in the town. The mayor is on hand to present a special award. Two wealthy sisters plan to make donations to the library—each hoping to outdo the other and win the award. The event begins cordially enough. But then secrets are revealed, and one of the sisters is found murdered.

Reed A. Lot, in his role as the detective/inspector, will keep a copy of the grid (table 8.1) and the time line (table 8.2) to keep the mystery on track.

TABLE 8.1
Grid for the Unfriendly Friends Script

Character	Motive
Prudence Modest	Sibling rivalry and competition
Coy N. Modest	Revenge for blackmail
Phil T. Rich	Greed, affair, Ira
Ira Rich	Betrayal by mother
Dee Kup	Greed and affair
Mayor I. M. Pompous	Revenge for teasing, power

TABLE 8.2
Time Line for the Unfriendly Friends Script

Time	Activities
7:00–7:05	Guests arrive and receive paperwork
7:05–7:30	Prudence and Coy bicker Vi and Rich argue Reed's welcome/mayor gives Reed letter Phil and Dee plot Mayor runs into Vi
7:30–7:45	Dee shows Ira note Prudence threatens Vi over check Dee confronts Coy about blackmail
7:50	Reed at podium; Vi found dead
7:55–8:00	Characters agitated, mingling
8:00–8:20	Reed opens mayor's letter Characters point fingers Phil reads blackmail letter/Phil and Coy fight Mayor notes red spot on Ira's shirt
8:20–8:40	Ira confronts Prudence Reed asks for audience help
8:45	Answer sheets collected 1. Crowd choice confesses 2. No consensus; Phil confesses

Characters

Each participating staff member or volunteer receives a description of the character he or she is depicting. They are responsible for portraying their character accurately, and in accordance with the time line of events. All should be good at improvisation and prepared to answer questions from guests.

Mrs. Vi L. Rich

She and Mrs. Prudence Modest are sisters. Their father was a multimillionaire who made his money breeding dung beetles. She is embarrassed by the nature of the family business but loves the profits. Mrs. Rich flaunts her money every chance she gets. She dresses in a gaudy yet well-to-do manner. She donates liberally, but only if she receives the credit she feels she is due—and a tax write-off. She has been known to walk out of functions without donating if she does not receive the amount of attention she believes is due her. At tonight's function, she intends to present a check for the largest amount ever donated to the library. Her husband is Mr. Phil T. Rich. Together they raised one son, Mr. Ira Rich. Unfortunately for her, Vi Rich will be the victim, stabbed in the back while powdering her nose.

Mrs. Prudence Modest

Mrs. Modest is Mrs. Rich's younger sister. She too has inherited millions and gives generously. Unlike her sister, however, she contributes quietly. Mrs. Modest serves on every board in town, loves to bake, and is seen as a pillar of the community—in public. Privately she is jealous of all the attention her sister receives. She recently heard her sister bad-mouthing their father and is extremely angry. This evening, she is determined to present the largest check ever to the library, no matter what it takes. She is married to Mr. Coy N. Modest, whom she adores in public but constantly derides when they are alone.

Mr. Phil T. Rich

Mr. Phil T. Rich clearly married his wife for her money, but he is smart enough to keep her happy. If she ever found out that he is having an affair with Dee Kup, he knows the divorce would be swift and severe. He can't let that happen. He is not too pleased that she is giving away so much money, nor is he happy about sharing her money with Ira Rich, the son they raised, knowing that Coy Modest is the young man's real father.

Mr. Coy N. Modest

Mr. Modest is a milquetoast. He lets everyone walk all over him. When he was a young man, he was seduced by his wife's sister, Vi, and they had a son, Ira Rich. Vi Rich has been blackmailing Coy ever since. Coy works for the city in the mayor's office because his wife has him on a budget. He needs this money to pay off Vi and keep his wife in the dark about Ira. Coy caters to Prudence's every whim, going to great lengths to try to impress her. He is afraid he'll get cut out of her will if she finds out about Ira. His secretary is Dee Kup.

Dee Kup

Dee is Phil T. Rich's mistress. She dresses somewhat provocatively, and she enjoys the good life. In fact, she'd like to marry Mr. Rich. Through her job as Coy Modest's secretary, Dee has discovered that Ira is Vi's and Coy's son and that Vi is blackmailing Coy. She wants Vi Rich out of the way before all of the money is gone—or before Phil T. Rich tires of her.

Mr. Ira Rich

Despite his upbringing, Ira is a nice guy, but very naive. He is in his early twenties and athletic, but is uncomfortable hanging out with the country club set. In college, he studied the role of insects in agriculture, in the hopes of taking over his grandfather's company and providing dung beetle colonies to developing countries. Ira is polite to his Aunt Prudence and "uncle" Coy. However, he does not get along well with his "father," Phil, who he thinks is running his grandfather's business into the ground. He is very interested in Dee Kup and likes to flirt with her. He has no idea that she is dating his "father," Phil. He also is not aware that Coy is his real father—until Dee tells him. At that point, he becomes outraged by his mother's betrayal.

Mayor I. M. Pompous

The mayor of Lazy River is a jolly, albeit conceited man. Even in a small town like Lazy River, he needed to resort to some dirty politicking to become mayor. Through the years, he has often forced Coy Modest to do his dirty work. He loves to meet and greet the citizens and adores attention and publicity. He's pleased to be presenting the philanthropy award this evening and is totally in his element in front of an audience, speaking to the press, and hobnobbing with socialites. The mayor has known Vi and Prudence since they were children. However, Vi always takes every opportunity to humiliate him for growing up poor. He would like nothing more than to avenge his bruised ego.

Mr. Reed A. Lot

Reed is the director of the Lazy River Public Library. He is a gregarious man who likes things neat and tidy. He is anxious to accept the donations from Vi Rich and Prudence Modest because the library's two branches are in need of renovation. He is willing to change the names of the branches to honor the donors and can't understand why the mayor is dead set against this idea. He will become the detective/inspector figure for the mystery.

Time Line

It is important that the characters refer to one another by name frequently and convey the nature of their relationships to one another clearly for the audience. Each event described below should happen separately, but in different parts of the room, so that the audience members do not miss anything.

7:00–7:05 p.m.

Guests arrive and receive a program. The characters are mingling and introducing themselves to the audience. Reed A. Lot encourages them to gather together or take their seats.

7:05–7:30 p.m.

Prudence and Coy Modest are quietly bickering in the front corner, with Prudence insisting to her husband that her sister, Vi, will not top her donation. Coy sheepishly takes a "yes, dear" attitude while trying to calm her. He claims he'll stand up to Vi and make sure she does not make a large donation.

Vi and Phil Rich are loudly arguing in the other front corner about their own donation. Vi wants to donate more than she planned to make sure she wins the philanthropy award. Phil doesn't think it's necessary to give all that money away and emphasizes that HER boy, Ira, would not approve.

From the podium, Reed welcomes everyone and is proud the library is able to host this event. He is looking forward to the evening even more than before, because he found out that there will be additional donations from members of the Friends of the Library. He thanks the guests for being there and singles out the mayor. Vi makes an audible snicker. Reed and the mayor shake hands, and the mayor slips Reed an envelope.

Prudence, Vi, and Coy mingle with the guests, intruding themselves. Coy stays away from Vi and stares angrily at her. Near the podium, Phil and Dee are amorous. They agree that Vi is spending money that they could use to be together. Phil is tired of supporting Ira too. He becomes angry and storms off. Dee is restless and distracted as she mingles with the audience.

The mayor accidentally bumps into Vi. Both are flustered yet indignant. The mayor reminds her that he is the powerful one now and will bring her down after years of humiliation. It's obvious they hate each other. The mayor keeps following Vi at a distance, glaring.

7:30–7:45 p.m.

Dee sees Ira and heads straight for him. She can't wait to tattle. Dee acts as if she is concerned about Ira, but is smug when she gives him a note she found on Coy's desk at work. It is a blackmail note from Vi to Coy. Ira is shocked, and Dee pretends to comfort him. Of course, she badmouths Vi. Ira gets mad and accidentally drops the note as he runs to find his mother. Dee talks aloud to herself that she hopes she will finally be rid of Vi for good.

Reed is at the head table with Prudence and Vi, showering them with praise for their generosity. As he walks away, Prudence catches Vi trying to see how much her donation check will be. Prudence gets mad and chases Vi out of the area, threatening her.

Dee confronts Coy. She mockingly tells him that she knows about the blackmail and that she told Ira about it. He is furious. They tussle a bit. Dee runs out, with Coy chasing her and calling her names.

7:50 p.m.

All of the main characters except Reed are out of sight. Reed is at the podium, beginning to discuss the history of the library. When a woman screams, Reed runs in that direction.

Reed returns to the podium, noticeably upset, and announces that Vi Rich has been murdered. She was stabbed in the back outside the ladies' restroom while powdering her nose. He asks that no one leave and takes charge of the investigation.

7:55–8:00 p.m.

All of the main characters (except Vi, of course) are mingling with one another in the presence of the audience. All are agitated. Phil looks disheveled. Ira is pacing. Prudence is henpecking Coy. Dee is shifty. The mayor seems nervous.

8:00–8:20 p.m.

Reed opens the envelope and reads the mayor's letter (see figure 8.2). He asks the mayor why he doesn't want the two library branches named after Vi Rich and Prudence Modest. The mayor is uncomfortable, and Prudence and Coy point out how much he has hated Vi since their childhood. The mayor seems defensive.

The characters start pointing fingers at each other and making accusations. Everyone is very animated. The mayor tries to use an audience member as a witness.

Phil finds the blackmail letter on the ground that Ira dropped (see figure 8.3) and directs his attention to Coy. Phil reads the letter out loud, sounding vindicated. Coy responds by announcing to everyone that Phil and Dee have been having an affair. Dee feigns betrayal. Phil takes a swing at Coy. Ira physically comes between them.

The mayor points out that Ira has a red spot on his sleeve. Dee insists it is blood. Ira says it must be lipstick. He says he confronted his mother (Vi) about the letter to Coy. She got upset and assured him the letter was a fake. She said he shouldn't believe rumors. She hugged him—which transferred the lipstick to his shirt—and said she was going to the ladies' room to freshen up. Ira claims that is the last time he saw his mother alive.

8:20–8:40 p.m.

Ira crossly asks Prudence what she knew about Vi and Coy. She bitterly replies that Vi was no good and got what was coming to her. She proclaims Coy useless and says Ira can have him.

Reed interrupts everyone and says he is not sure who killed Vi. He asks for the audience's help and encourages questions. Audience members can look at evidence. The characters again plead their innocence to the audience and look for support, alibis, and anything else that seems relevant.

Mr. Reed A. Lot
Lazy River Public Library
Lazy River, AB 11111

Dear Mr. Lot,

It was a pleasure talking to you last week. It's good to know your wife is doing well.

Your stewardship of the library has been most impressive. I am glad the funds have been raised to renovate the Northpointe and Southside branches. I have some serious concerns, however, about your idea to rename the branches in honor of Vi Rich and Prudence Modest. Perhaps this is something we should discuss.

Please call me tomorrow afternoon, and we can talk about the matter.

Sincerely,
Mayor I. M. Pompous

FIGURE 8.2
Mayor's Letter Concerning Vi and Prudence

When the interaction with the audience fades a bit or they begin to form a consensus opinion about who murdered Vi, Reed asks everyone to fill out the answer sheet they were given when they came in. Characters should begin pointing fingers at one another again.

8:45 p.m.

After collecting the answer sheets, Reed looks through them.

1. If one name clearly stands out, he should accuse that character of the murder. At that time, the other characters should start to encircle the guilty party and he or she will reluctantly confess. Reed will grab that character by the arm and say he's taking them to the police.

Once Reed and the guilty party have exited, the other characters should act relieved and congratulate the audience. Reed, Vi, and the murderer can rejoin everyone in five minutes.

Coy—

Your payments really are totally insufficient. What kind of father are you?

Pru will run you out of town when she finds out about our love child.

I can hardly wait!

Vi

FIGURE 8.3

Blackmail Note

2. If there is no consensus as to the murderer, Reed will poll the audience by asking them to raise their hand if they think a certain person is guilty while pointing to each character. (Characters can raise their hands too, which adds to the fun.)

Once Reed has polled the audience, Phil should try to run away, but Coy and the mayor will capture him. Dee shouts after him, "Darling, no!"

Phil confesses that when he heard Vi tell Ira that there was no blackmail and that it was just a rumor that Coy was his father, he snapped. Phil says he killed Vi in a rage when he realized their plan to frame Ira was not going to work. Reed leads Phil away with Dee following, crying.

The other characters comfort Ira, then mingle with the audience. Reed, Vi, and Phil can rejoin everyone in 5 minutes.

Answer Sheet

Encourage audience members to take notes as the mystery progresses, and be sure to leave enough room for them to do so.

Circle the name of the person you think murdered Mrs. Vi L. Rich:

Mrs. Prudence Modest

Mr. Coy N. Modest

Ms. Dee Kup

Mayor I. M. Pompous

Mr. Phil T. Rich

Mr. Ira Rich

CHAPTER NINE

DEDUCTION SCRIPT

MERLIN'S MINIONS MYSTERY

Mysteries can be used to encourage patrons to expand their minds. By immersing patrons in legends and literature, we can open whole new worlds to them figuratively and literally. We can pique their curiosity and introduce them to places, characters, and themes that will educate or entertain them for a lifetime.

The theme for this mystery is fantasy. This can encompass settings like Camelot, Neverland, and Oz. Within these venues, of course, there are magical beings and mythical creatures. The motivation is to tap into the patrons' imagination while familiarizing them with library resources and research skills. Costumes, props, and music are particularly helpful and encouraged for this mystery, and make it that much more entertaining. Also, a fabulous atmosphere can be created by imitating scenes such as Merlin's Tower laboratory, a burrow for the Lost Boys, or the Emerald City.

The premise of the mystery is twofold. Initially patrons are told that they are learning to become wizards. Later, it is revealed that a portal has been opened through which fabulous and sometimes dangerous creatures such as dragons, unicorns, mermaids, and fairies have entered our world. In order to return these beings to their respective fantasy lands, the patrons, as amateur wizards, must determine who stole Merlin's crystal ball. A similar mystery could be hosted involving Alice in Wonderland, Robin Hood, Oz, Narnia, or just about any other fantasy world—especially those in the public domain. If you would like to use characters or text from published work that is still in copyright, you must obtain permission to do so.

The mystery begins with teams of patrons receiving packets, including a summary or backstory of a fantasy land, and their first clue. They must take their answers to the reference librarian (Merlin), or another costumed

TABLE 9.1

Grid for the Merlin's Minions Script

Phoenix	Cyclops	Dragon	Fairie	Unicorn	Gnome
D&D	Carmina Burana	Sorcerer's Apprentice	Wizard101	CT Yankee	Harry Potter
Harry Potter	D&D	Carmina Burana	Sorcerer's Apprentice	Wizard101	CT Yankee
CT Yankee	Harry Potter	D&D	Carmina Burana	Sorcerer's Apprentice	Wizard101
Wizard101	CT Yankee	Harry Potter	D&D	Carmina Burana	Sorcerer's Apprentice
Sorcerer's Apprentice	Wizard101	CT Yankee	Harry Potter	D&D	Carmina Burana
Carmina Burana	Sorcerer's Apprentice	Wizard101	CT Yankee	Harry Potter	D&D
Ref Librarian	Ref Librarian	Ref Librarian	Ref Librarian	Ref Librarian	Ref Librarian
Book letters	Book Letters	Book Letters	Book Letters	Book Letters	Book Letters
Circulation	Circulation	Circulation	Circulation	Circulation	Circulation
Crystal ball stolen!	Crystal ball stolen!	Crystal ball stolen!	Crystal ball stolen!	Crystal ball stolen!	Crystal ball stolen!
Evidence and answer sheet	Evidence and answer sheet	Evidence and answer sheet	Evidence and answer sheet	Evidence and answer sheet	Evidence and answer sheet
Meeting room	Meeting room	Meeting room	Meeting room	Meeting room	Meeting room
Portal closed	Portal closed	Portal closed	Portal closed	Portal closed	Portal closed

character, in order to get their next clue. Not only does this familiarize patrons with the librarians and staff, but it also immerses them in the mystery.

As you can see on the grid in table 9.1, once patrons complete the initial clues, they report to the reference librarian. The librarian gives each team a letter from Merlin informing the participants that they have successfully completed the first step to becoming wizards. The letter also instructs them to locate specific books in the library that teach them more about spells and magical powers. Choose actual titles in your library with wonderfully fanciful names. Prior to the mystery, place small slips of paper containing additional evidence regarding the theft of the crystal ball in these books.

After the teams retrieve their books and gather at the circulation desk, an announcement is made: a portal has been opened and fantastic beasts and mythical beings are on the loose. In order to reopen the portal and return them to their homelands, patrons must determine who stole Merlin's crystal ball. (For a bit of drama, have a dragon run by or a Cyclops on the loose!) The librarian portraying one of the characters (preferably Merlin) uses his or her powers to put a spell on the books, at which time the existence of the new evidence in the books is revealed. Teams are given an answer sheet and instructions on where to meet once they have determined who took the crystal ball. The teams use the new evidence slips, in addition to any other information they have gathered, to solve the mystery.

Once everyone meets to discuss their solutions, Merlin is able to recover the crystal ball. He summons the power to round up the creatures and sends them back through the portal. You may conduct a ceremony to bestow magical powers on some or all of the participants. Prizes can be awarded, and refreshments, such as Merlin Munchies, Cyclops Cider, and Pixie Stix, can be served.

Some passages in the script that follows are explanations directed to you. These are all italicized.

Introduction

This is best spoken by the reference librarian, preferably as Merlin.

Good evening. I am Merlin, prophet, magician, and advisor to the legendary King Arthur. I am pleased to be your host for this most mysterious and adventurous evening. Allow me to introduce to you my colleagues [name other costumed characters].

As you may know, some magical beings are born, while others are created. For example, some wizards—good and evil—are gifted with powers at the moment of their conception, while others acquire their powers through a twist of fate, a chance encounter, or after a period of apprenticeship. We are glad that you have joined us this evening to see if you may indeed have what it takes to become a wizard yourself.

Since you have come here of your own volition and were not formally chosen, there are a few tasks we need you to perform so that you may prove yourself qualified to become a wizard. So, let us begin with your first exercise, and do take care, because strange and exciting events await you on your journey.

Summary

Include this in each team's packet, along with their first clue.

One of the most famous enchanted places ever imagined is Camelot, the principal city in King Arthur's realm. It is an idyllic place where the virtues of truth, loyalty, courage, wisdom, and purity are highly valued. In a meeting room within the castle is the Round Table, around which all of the king's knights are seated as equals. Merlin is one of the oldest and most powerful wizards ever known. He advises King Arthur in his military ventures, as well as in his quest for the Holy Grail.

Many legends have been passed down about Camelot since medieval times. Its historical roots lie in the British Isles and their history. In addition to Merlin are these notable inhabitants of Camelot:

King Arthur—king of the Britons

Queen Guinevere—Arthur's wife; had an affair with Lancelot

Morgause—Arthur's half-sister; mother to Gawain and Mordred

Mordred—Son of Morgause and Arthur; traitor who kills and is killed by Arthur

Sir Lancelot—knight; raised by Lady-of-the-Lake; had affair with Guinevere

Sir Galahad—knight; son of Lancelot and Elaine; attains the Holy Grail

Sir Gawain—knight; son of Morgause and King Lot

Sir Percival—knight; reaches Grail Castle but fails to attain the Holy Grail

Sir Dagonet—knight; King Arthur's court jester

Morgan le Fey—Arthur's sister; studied magic under Merlin

Elaine of Carbonek—seduced Lancelot by pretending to be Guinevere; Galahad's mother

Lady-of-the-Lake—gave Excalibur to Arthur; enchanted Merlin; brought dying Arthur to Avalon

Patrons will find these resources most useful in answering the clues and finding their books:

- www.wizards.com
- www.mugglenet.com
- library catalog
- www.wizard101.com
- en.wikipedia.org
- www.imdb.com

Print each of these clues on a separate piece of paper for each team. Label the envelopes and place them in the proper locations. Note that the reference librarian gives out each clue after being shown the correct answer to the previous clue.

D&D CLUE

On the Dungeons and Dragon's official website, www.wizards.com, under "What is D&D?":

a. Who or what is the DM? _____

b. What does the DM play? _____

HARRY POTTER CLUE

Who once said to a young wizard, "It is our choices, Harry, that show what we truly are, far more than our abilities."

a. Speaker's name: _____

b. From what book? _____

CT YANKEE CLUE

Who wrote the 1889 novel *A Connecticut Yankee in King Arthur's Court?*

_____

WIZARD 101 CLUE

What is the name of the comic featured on the www.wizard101.com homepage?

_____

SORCERER CLUE

"Mirror, mirror on the wall, who's the most famous sorcerer's apprentice of all?"

a.   His/her name is _____

b.   From what 1940 film? _____

CARMINA BURANA CLUE

In what 1981 movie does "O Fortuna" from *Carmina Burana* provide the background music as King Arthur's knights prepare for battle? (According to the Internet Movie Database, it is the only piece featured on the movie's soundtrack that is not by Richard Wagner.)

Answer Key

D&D
   a. Dungeon Master
   b. The "bad guys"

Harry Potter quote:
   a. Albus Dumbledore
   b. *Harry Potter and the Chamber of Secrets*

CT Yankee
   Mark Twain

Wizard101
   Abracadoodle

Sorcerer's Apprentice
   a. Mickey Mouse
   b. *Fantasia*

Carmina Burana
   Excalibur

Merlin's Letter

Try to find books in your collection that have fun fantasy or wizard-like titles. Make a separate letter for each team listing three different books for them to find. Place the evidence slips in the books and reshelve them before the mystery. Each set of three books should contain one full set of evidence slips.

---

§ Camelot §

Dear _____ team,

Congratulations on correctly answering the clues. You have been accepted into wizard apprenticeship!

For this phase of your training, you will need to familiarize yourself with manuscripts containing powerful wisdom.

Accordingly, please locate the following books and bring them to the circulation desk:

So You Want to Be a Wizard?
Dragons and Dragon Lore
Witches and Warlocks: Tales of Black Magic, Old and New

Yours sincerely,
Merlin

Merlin's Emergency Announcement

This announcement is made once all teams have collected their books.

I am afraid some terrible events have occurred! A portal has been opened through which fabulous—though sometimes dangerous—creatures, such as dragons, unicorns, Cyclops, mermaids, and fairies, have entered our world. They are loose, they are lost, and some are becoming agitated.

In order to return them to their respective fantasy lands, I will need my crystal ball. But my crystal ball has been stolen. As amateur wizards, you must help to determine who stole it. Retrieving the crystal ball is the only way we can reopen the portal and send these beasts and fanciful creatures back to the lands where they belong.

Please, bring me your books.

Merlin proceeds to place a spell on each team's collection of books. He tells the teams that the books now contain slips that give a time line of evidence as to when the portal was opened. He implores the teams to help him determine who opened the portal.

Teams are given the summary containing the list of characters from Camelot, along with an answer sheet. They are instructed to gather in the meeting room once they have determined who stole the crystal ball.

Evidence Slips

There are fifteen evidence statements that can be cut into strips. Before the mystery, place five slips randomly in each team's three books and reshelve the books. Each team must receive an identical set of fifteen slips.

The crystal ball was reported stolen at 10:30 p.m. by the Lady-of-the-Lake.

Queen Guinevere, Sir Galahad, and Sir Percival recalled seeing the crystal ball on the table at 10:15 p.m.

At 10:21 p.m. King Arthur scolded Mordred for grappling with Sir Gawain.

Merlin stopped Mordred as he was trying to leave. Mordred was searched, but there was no trace of the crystal ball.

King Arthur was showing his sword, Excalibur, to Sir Galahad at 10:28 p.m.

Morgan le Fey said she saw Sir Lancelot walking by the table at 10:27 p.m.

At 10:30 p.m., the Knights of the Round Table were celebrating a toast.

When King Arthur summoned Sir Dagonet, the jester said, "Please do not be angry with me, sire. I tried to stop her."

Morgause was angry that Queen Guinevere asked her to accompany her to the balcony at 10:28 p.m. because she would have liked to have caught whoever stole the crystal ball herself.

Elaine of Carbonek heard Morgause and Queen Guinevere arguing at 10:29 p.m.

Sir Percival saw Morgause and Mordred laughing together at 10:18 p.m.

> Morgan le Fey asked Sir Gawain to remove a drunken Mordred from the castle at 10:19 p.m.
>
> Sir Lancelot boasted to Queen Guinevere that he could slay any dragon that got out of control.
>
> At 10:10 p.m., Arthur's sisters complained to Sir Dagonet about what boring parties Queen Guinevere hosts.
>
> Merlin assured King Arthur that the portal can only be opened or closed by using the crystal ball.

Diversion

Use this exercise if you need to stall for time as you wait for all of the teams to arrive at the circulation desk. Or you might have the patrons mingle with the staff/characters before all teams arrive.

Now that you have proven yourselves adept at using the library, you'll have to demonstrate a bit of knowledge about the legend of King Arthur.

Go to the following website: www.funtrivia.com/playquizquiz2306631a69050.html

Take the quiz, print your answer sheet, and bring your results back to the circulation desk.

Answer Sheet

In the back of your books, you will find evidence slips to analyze. Combine the information on the slips with the information you have already collected to answer the following:

Who took the crystal ball? _____

Gather your team and bring this completed form to the meeting room to continue the mystery . . .

More than one team might correctly solve the mystery, but that is okay. Have the team(s) with the right answer guess where the crystal ball might be.

Answer: Morgan le Fey

CHAPTER TEN

TWEEN PATRON SCRIPT

TREASURE ISLAND MYSTERY

This mystery is geared toward patrons who are in middle school or junior high school. The theme for the mystery is pirates, and the mystery focuses on the book *Treasure Island* and the Pirates of the Caribbean film series. It also refers to other well-known fictional and real pirates. This mystery may be used as a library orientation, as a young adult event, or perhaps in connection with a literature or social studies class.

The goals of this mystery are to show students how to use library resources and make them more familiar with their librarian. While some middle and junior high schools and public libraries have access to Google, Ask.com, Yahoo! and other major search engines, other libraries have a few databases available, mostly through EBSCOhost. This mystery attempts to provide clues that make use of different types of resources. As always, you can tailor the questions to fit your particular library's situation. It is important to include some details regarding information literacy, since this helps students understand and evaluate their sources.

The students are to bring each sheet to the librarian or their teacher (or both) once they have answered the clue. The librarian will check their answers and then give them the next clue. It is easiest to put the clues in the proper order ahead of time according to the grid in table 10.1. Most of the clues are intended to be answered using a computer. For this reason, the order of the clues is not as important because the students will not be competing for the same resources. If you do not have enough computers, conduct the mystery with fewer teams.

One thing we noticed when hosting mysteries for younger age groups is that these patrons tend to misread or fail to completely read the clues before attempting to answer them. This often leads to an incorrect answer initially, but it is a good teaching opportunity for the librarian or teacher. Be sure to stress to the students that they understand what the clues are asking, so that they do not become frustrated.

The students will begin with a treasure map, a summary of the first few chapters of *Treasure Island,* a pencil, and a flashlight. Once they successfully answer all of the clues, they are given a crossword puzzle to complete using their answers to the clues (see figure 10.1). The crossword puzzle sets up an anagram (see figure 10.2). By deciphering the anagram, the students are prompted to seek a globe (or map or atlas, or something similar) where they find a treasure chest. The actual treasure should be something fun like chocolate candy coins, trinkets, or even paperback copies of *Treasure Island.*

Be creative. Perhaps put the treasure chest at a particular longitude and latitude. Or have the students find a key that opens an actual wooden chest full of goodies. Have everyone dress like pirates. Through their quest to find buried treasure, the students will learn research skills and familiarity with their library along the way.

Some passages in the script that follows are explanations directed to you. These are all italicized.

Introduction

Welcome to the library! It's a good thing you have joined us today, because there is treasure to be found! Everyone likes to search for buried treasure, don't they? But you and I both know that where there is a treasure, there usually are pirates.

In fact, I bet you don't even realize that there are pirates all around. How many of you have seen any of the Pirates of the Caribbean movies? Johnny Depp was Jack Sparrow, right? And how about *Peter Pan*? Of course, there was Captain Hook. The Sea Captain, Horatio McCallister, is a character on *The Simpsons*. You can even eat seafood at a restaurant called Long John Silver's. Do you know where they got the name of that restaurant? Long John Silver is one of the main characters in the book *Treasure Island* by Robert Louis Stevenson.

TABLE 10.1
Grid for the Treasure Island Script

SHIP: Adventure Galley CAPTAIN: William Kidd	SHIP: Royal Fortune CAPTAIN: Black Bart	SHIP: Martha's Revenge CAPTAIN: Trader Jack	SHIP: The Pride CAPTAIN: Jean Lafitte	SHIP: Ship O Ghouls CAPTAIN: Patchy the Pirate
1	2	3	4	5
2	3	4	5	6
3	4	5	6	7
4	5	6	7	8
5	6	7	8	9
6	7	8	9	10
7	8	9	10	11
8	9	10	11	12
9	10	11	12	1
10	11	12	1	2
11	12	1	2	3
12	1	2	3	4
Crossword	Crossword	Crossword	Crossword	Crossword
Anagram	Anagram	Anagram	Anagram	Anagram
Treasure	Treasure	Treasure	Treasure	Treasure

Today we are going to follow clues left by pirates in order to find our own treasure. Shiver me timbers! It's a dangerous mission, but if you're up to it, you will be rewarded. Are you ready?

I have a packet of information for each team. When I tell you to start, read the summary of the first few chapters of the book *Treasure Island*. That will set the stage for our treasure hunt today.

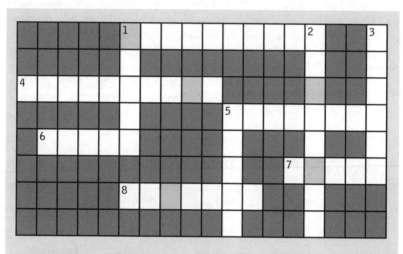

ACROSS

1. National Football League team's pirate mascot
4. Name of Jim Hawkins's ship
5. Robert Louis Stevenson's birthplace
6. Actor who played Muppets' Long John Silver
7. Blackbeard's real name, Edward _____
8. Grace O'Malley visited the queen of this country

DOWN

1. Female pirate Anne _____
2. Captain of the *Hispaniola*
3. "Black Sam's" shipwreck
5. Keira Knightley portrayed Elizabeth _____ in the Pirates of the Caribbean series

FIGURE 10.1

Treasure Island Crossword Puzzle

Summary

Include this in the students' packets along with the treasure map.

In the book *Treasure Island,* an old pirate, Billy Bones, is living at the Admiral Benbow Inn, a lodging house run by young Jim Hawkins and his parents. The old pirate is a drunkard who scares many of the inn's guests. Shortly before Bones dies, he tells tales of his days as a pirate and warns Jim to watch out for a one-legged sailor.

Thinking quickly, Jim secretly takes the key to Bones's old sea chest and removes a packet. He and his mother flee to Squire Trelawney's residence, where they meet with Dr. Livesey. There they open Bones's packet and discover that it contains the map to Captain John Flint's Treasure Island. Trelawney, Livesey, and Jim make plans to set sail with Captain Smollett on a treasure-hunting voyage. In his excitement, however, Trelawney makes a critical mistake: He hires Long John Silver, a one-legged pirate, to be the ship's cook.

					1 B	U	C	C	A	N	E	E	R	2 S			3 W
					O									M			H
4 H	I	S	P	A	N	I	O	L	A					O			Y
					N					5 S	C	O	T	L	A	N	D
	6 C	U	R	R	Y					W				L			A
										A			7 T	E	A	C	H
					8 E	N	G	L	A	N	D			T			
										N				T			

Use the shaded letters to solve this anagram:

____ ____ ____ ____ ____

Where this item is located, you will find your last clue.

FIGURE 10.2

Completed Treasure Island Crossword Puzzle and Anagram

After they set sail for Treasure Island, Jim overhears Silver and other crewmen plotting to take over the ship once the treasure is on board. Jim, Captain Smollett, and the other sailors can't find the treasure without the help of the experienced seafaring pirates—but they may lose their lives if they discover the gold, jewels, and riches beyond their wildest dreams on Treasure Island.

Your mission is also to find hidden treasure. You've been given a ship, a crew, and a map, shown in figure 10.3 (because every treasure hunt needs a map). You must follow the clues to arrive at the site of the treasure first.

These are the resources that patrons will be directed to or will find most useful in answering the clues:

- online or traditional encyclopedia
- WorldCat
- www.imdb.com
- www.kidsclick.org
- teacher.scholastic.com
- www.nationalgeographic.com
- Kids Search database (EBSCOhost)
- bestoflegends.org
- disney.go.com
- online or traditional thesaurus
- www.historicbeaufort.com
- library catalog
- www.amazon.com
- *Treasure Island*

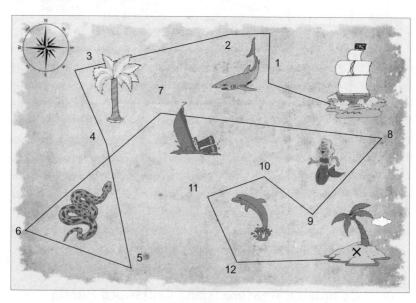

FIGURE 10.3

A Treasure Map to Make the Mystery Realistic

CLUE 1

Robert Louis Stevenson is the author of *Treasure Island*. Use an encyclopedia and find the entry for Robert Louis Stevenson.

a.   In what year was Stevenson born? _____

b.   In what year did Stevenson die? _____

c.   In what country was Stevenson born? _____

Show your answers to the librarian to get your next clue.

CLUE 2

According to the Internet Movie Database (www.imdb.com), what actor portrayed Long John Silver in the 1996 movie *Muppet Treasure Island*?

_____

Show your answer to the librarian to get your next clue.

CLUE 3

In research, it is important to use good sources. Scholastic is a reputable publishing company. It published the Harry Potter series. It also publishes *Upfront,* a teen magazine.

Go to http://teacher.scholastic.com/scholasticnews/indepth/upfront/index.asp.

Under Student Activities, search for "Treasure Island." Click on the book review.

What is the name of the ship Jim is sailing on?

_____

Show your answer to the librarian to get your next clue.

CLUE 4

Using the Kids Search database (in EBSCOhost), search for "Treasure Island." (*Note: only libraries that subscribe to EBSCO can access this site.*) Narrow the results by the subject "Treasure Island (book)." Use the PDF full text of the article "X marks the spot," to answer the following questions about the book:

a. Who is the protagonist? _____

b. Who is the antagonist? _____

Show your answers to the librarian to get your next clue.

CLUE 5

Use a thesaurus to find other words for "pirate."

_____

_____

_____

_____

    Based on this information, what two cities' National Football League teams' mascots are pirates?

a. _____

b. _____

Show your answers to the librarian to get your next clue.

CLUE 6

According to the official Disney website for Pirates of the Caribbean, what character does Keira Knightley portray in *Curse of the Black Pearl*, *Dead Man's Chest*, and *At World's End*?

_____

Show your answer to the librarian to get your next clue.

CLUE 7

Beaufort is a city in North Carolina where the infamous pirate Blackbeard lived.

Go to www.historicbeaufort.com.

a. According to Blackbeard's Tale, what was Blackbeard's original name?

_____

b. What was the name of Blackbeard's ship?

_____

Show your answers to the librarian to get your next clue.

CLUE 8

Using the online catalog, find the call number for the book *Treasure Island*. Locate the book in the library.

What is the call number of the book? _____

According to chapter XXVII, what phrase does Long John Silver's green parrot, Captain Flint, frequently repeat? _____

Show your answers to the librarian to get your next clue.

CLUE 9

There were female pirates on the high seas. For example, find the book *Sisters of the Sea* on Amazon.com. What are the names of the two women pirates in the subtitle of the book? (You may use WorldCat if your library has access to that service.)

_____

Show your answers to the librarian to get your next clue.

CLUE 10

When you search the Internet, always make sure to use a source with a good reputation. This will ensure that the information you receive is accurate, especially since anyone can post anything on the Internet.

Go to this website created by librarians: www.kidsclick.org. Under "Facts and Reference," click on "Dictionaries." Using the *American Heritage Dictionary*, look up the following pirate lingo and write the definitions here:

a.   jolly roger _____

b.   crow's nest _____

c.   Davy Jones's locker _____

Show your answers to the librarian to get your next clue.

CLUE 11

Search Google for the pirate ship *Whydah*. If you search just the name in Google, you will get about 142,000 hits. If you search for *pirate ship Whydah*, you will get approximately 15,700 hits because the browser will look for every instance of the word *pirate* and the word *ship* and the word *Whydah*. If you search for "pirate ship Whydah" (in quotes), you get only 3,610 hits, which is still a lot, but much more precise because you searched for a phrase. This is one way to narrow your search results.

According to the article on the website for *National Geographic*:

a.   Who was the captain of the *Whydah*? _____

b.   In what year was the ship's bell recovered? _____

Show your answers to the librarian to get your next clue.

CLUE 12

Legend has it there was a female pirate from Ireland who led over 200 men. Her Gaelic name was Gráinne Ni Mháille. She is known to us today as Grace O'Malley. Many songs, books, a play, and even a movie tell the story her life.

According to http://bestoflegends.org/pirates/grainne.html, Grace met with the monarch of what country in 1593?

Show your answers to the librarian to get your next clue.

Answer Key

1a. 1850
1b. 1894
1c. Scotland
 2. Tim Curry
 3. *Hispaniola*
4a. Jim Hawkins
4b. Long John Silver
 5. marauder, corsair, buccaneer, raider, privateer
5a/b. Tampa Bay Buccaneers and Oakland Raiders
 6. Elizabeth Swann
7a. Edward Teach
7b. *The Queen Anne's Revenge*
 8. STEVENSON; "Pieces of eight"
 9. Anne Bonny and Mary Read
10a. A black flag bearing the emblematic white skull and crossbones of a pirate ship
10b. A small lookout platform near the top of a ship's mast
10c. A grave at the bottom of the sea
11a. Samuel "Black Sam" Bellamy
11b. 1985
 12. England

RESOURCES

Boykin, Amy W., and Willson-Metzger, Alicia. "A Murder in the Library." *Virginia Libraries* 51, no. 4 (October 2005): 20–22. *Library, Information Science and Technology Abstracts,* EBSCOhost (accessed August 5, 2008).

Karle, Elizabeth M. "Invigorating the Library Experience: Creative Programming Ideas." *College and Research Libraries News* 69, no. 3 (March 2008): 141–144.

Kasbohm, Kristine E., Schoen, David, and Dubaj, Michelle. "Launching the Library Mystery Tour: A Library Component for the 'First-Year Experience.'" *College and Undergraduate Libraries* 13, no. 2 (December 2006): 35–46. *Library, Information Science and Technology Abstracts,* EBSCOhost (accessed August 5, 2008).

Marcus, Sandra, and Beck, Sheila. "A Library Adventure: Comparing a Treasure Hunt with a Traditional Freshman Orientation Tour." *College and Research Libraries* 64, no. 1 (January 2003): 23–44. *Library, Information Science and Technology Abstracts,* EBSCOhost (accessed August 5, 2008).

Wilmer, Kathryn G. "Mystery at the Library." *School Library Journal* 28, no. 9 (May 1982): 24. *Library, Information Science and Technology Abstracts,* EBSCOhost (accessed August 5, 2008).

INDEX

You may also be interested in

Quick and Popular Reads for Teens: For more than ten years YALSA has produced two annual lists, Popular Paperbacks for Young Adults and Quick Picks for Reluctant Readers, consisting of recommended reading targeted at young adults who are not avid readers. *Quick and Popular Reads for Teens* compiles bibliographic information about the books honored by these two lists. Make choosing titles for teens fun, quick, and easy with this one-of-a-kind resource!

Creating the Customer-Driven Academic Library: With more and more scholarly content available online and accessible almost anywhere, where does the traditional "brick and mortar" library fit in? In this book Jeannette Woodward confronts this and other pressing issues facing today's academic librarians. Her trailblazing strategies center on keeping the customer's point of view in focus at all times to help you keep customers coming through the door.

Multicultural Programs for Tweens and Teens is a one-stop resource that encourages children and young adults to explore different cultures. The fifty flexible programming ideas allow you to choose a program specific to your scheduling needs; create an event that reflects a specific culture; and recommend further resources to tweens and teens interested in learning more about diverse cultures.

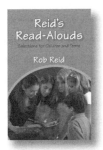

Reid's Read-Alouds: Rob Reid makes reading fun and exciting with passages from two hundred titles in high-interest topics, encompassing fiction and nonfiction; advice on how to prepare for a read-aloud; a subject index to make program planning easier; and bibliographic information on all titles. You will find plenty to engage your audiences and reinvigorate programs in this time-saving resource!

Check out these and other great titles at www.alastore.ala.org